OCCASION

Hungary: Economic Policies for Sustainable Growth

Carlo Cottarelli, Thomas Krueger, Reza Moghadam,
Perry Perone, Edgardo Ruggiero, and Rachel van Elkan

INTERNATIONAL MONETARY FUND
Washington DC
February 1998

© 1998 International Monetary Fund

Composition: Alicia Etchebarne-Bourdin

Cataloging-in-Publication Data

Hungary : economic policies for sustainable growth / Carlo Cottarelli . . .
[et al.]—Washington, DC : International Monetary Fund, 1998

     p. cm.—(Occasional paper ; ISSN 0251-6365 ; 159)

ISBN 1-55775-709-7

    1. Hungary—Economic policy—1989. 2. Economic stabilization—
Hungary. 3. Hungary—Economic conditions—1989. 4. International
Monetary Fund—Hungary. I. Cottarelli, Carlo. II. Occasional paper
(International Monetary Fund) ; no. 159.

HC300.283.H85 1998

Price: US$18.00
(US$15.00 to full-time faculty members and
students at universities and colleges)

Please send orders to:
International Monetary Fund, Publication Services
700 19th Street, N.W., Washington, D.C. 20431, U.S.A.
Tel.: (202) 623-7430   Telefax: (202) 623-7201
E-mail: publications@imf.org
Internet: http://www.imf.org

recycled paper

Contents

Boxes

Chapter

Tables

Chapter

Figures

Chapter

The following symbols have been used throughout this paper:

. . .   to indicate that data are not available;

—   to indicate that the figure is zero or less than half the final digit shown, or that the item does not exist;

–   between years or months (e.g., 1994–95 or January–June) to indicate the years or months covered, including the beginning and ending years or months;

/   between years (e.g., 1994/95) to indicate a crop or fiscal (financial) year.

"Billion" means a thousand million.

Minor discrepancies between constituent figures and totals are due to rounding.

The term "country," as used in this paper, does not in all cases refer to a territorial entity that is a state as understood by international law and practice; the term also covers some territorial entities that are not states, but for which statistical data are maintained and provided internationally on a separate and independent basis.

Preface

This occasional paper is a collection of studies focusing on economic developments in Hungary, particularly during 1995–97, a period of momentous changes for the Hungarian economy. Most of these studies were prepared as background material for discussions between the International Monetary Fund and the Hungarian authorities during the last two years, while a precautionary Stand-By Arrangement (which expired on February 14, 1998) was in place.

The paper benefited from comments from László Akar, Mark Allen, Lajos Bokros, Zoltán Bosze, Ákos Cserés, Peter Doyle, Peter Isard, Csaba László, Leslie Lipschitz, György Sándor, György Szapáry, Tamás Tétényi, Szilvia Zádor, and other members of the staff of the National Bank of Hungary and the Ministry of Finance of Hungary, as well as from participants in seminars held at the Universitá "La Sapienza" of Rome and the National Bank of Croatia, including Marcello De Cecco, Domenico Mario Nuti, and Marko Škreb. The authors are also grateful to Sándor Czirják, Jean-Jacques Dethier, Tibor Draskovics, George Kopits, Álmos Kovács, Judith Neményi, Werner Riecke, Roberto Rocha, Massimo Russo, and György Surányi for comments and views received during the course of the last two years on some of the topics of this paper. They would also like to thank Patricia Emerson and Indra Perera for secretarial assistance. Martha Bonilla of the External Relations Department edited the manuscripts and coordinated production of the publication. David Maxwell provided excellent research assistance.

The views expressed here are those of the authors and do not necessarily reflect the opinions of other members of the IMF staff or its Executive Directors.

I Introduction

Carlo Cottarelli

The process of macroeconomic adjustment and structural reform in Hungary during 1995–97 deserves attention for several reasons.

- First, the performance of the Hungarian economy improved dramatically during this period, correcting some long-standing macroeconomic imbalances that had deepened through 1994.

- Second, this improvement reflected primarily a consistent set of macroeconomic and structural policies implemented by the authorities, rather than favorable external developments. Thus, there are important lessons to be learned for other countries facing macroeconomic imbalances.

- Third, while the process of macroeconomic adjustment and convergence toward European market economies is not yet over, an important phase in the transition can be regarded as completed. This phase was initiated with the economic adjustment package enacted in March 1995, and has continued with the support of a precautionary Stand-By Arrangement with the IMF during March 1996–February 1998.

During this period, several momentous steps in the integration of the Hungarian economy with the rest of Europe and the industrial countries community have taken place. In May 1996, Hungary acceded to the Organization for Economic Cooperation and Development (OECD); in July 1997, it was invited to join the North Atlantic Treaty Organization (NATO); and, in the same month, the European Commission recommended that the European Union (EU) start membership talks in the near future. These steps cast future economic developments and issues in Hungary in a new perspective. While economic developments are never characterized by quantum leaps, the end of the Stand-By Arrangement with the IMF provides a symbolic turning point in Hungary's recent economic history.

This paper is organized as follows. After providing a bird's-eye view of economic developments in Hungary before the March 1995 stabilization, Chapter II discusses the main features of the stabilization package, outlines the macroeconomic and structural policies that characterized 1995–97, and describes the outcome of those policies. The chapters that follow can ideally—and somewhat schematically—be grouped under two headings: Chapters III–VII deal with "macroeconomic" issues, while Chapters VIII–XII focus on "structural" issues.

Four main macroeconomic issues are explored. Chapter III looks at Hungary's external balance and at the appropriate contribution to investment that, in such a country, should come from external saving. This is a key issue, as historically, Hungary's external debt has been high and has often constrained the country's growth potential during the 1990s. Chapters IV and V focus on the fiscal balance, describing the process of fiscal consolidation during 1995–97, outlining the main structural measures undertaken in the fiscal area, and assessing the areas where further reform appears to be needed. Chapter VI deals with growth. In Hungary, the output shock related to the collapse of central planning was not as severe as in other transition economies. The subsequent recovery had, until recently, also been more modest. The chapter discusses the factors behind this performance and looks at Hungary's growth potential in the medium term. The last chapter on macroeconomic issues, Chapter VII, looks at inflation. One achievement of the 1995–97 adjustment program is that, despite a sizable up-front depreciation of the forint and increases in administered prices, the increase in inflation was only temporary: indeed inflation fell below 20 percent in 1997, which had rarely happened during the 1990s. Progress has been less rapid, however, in the most recent period. Chapter VII also discusses the factors that sustained inflation in the 1990s and looks at the prospects for disinflation in the future.

The structural chapters focus on goods, labor, and financial markets. Chapters VIII and IX deal with two developments that have increased competitiveness and the medium-term growth potential of the Hungarian economy: privatization (mostly through the sale of enterprises to foreign investors) and the increased openness of the economy. Chapter X focuses on the labor market, discussing its degree of flexibility compared with other transition and nontransition economies, and highlighting the rigidities arising from overly generous and poorly targeted social programs. Chapters XI and XII discuss the factors behind increased competition and efficiency in financial markets, including the recent strengthening of the banking system, and the progressive liberalization of the capital account of the balance of payments. Finally, Chapter XIII looks at the policy agenda for the future.

II Macroeconomic and Structural Adjustment During 1995–97: An Overview

Carlo Cottarelli

Economic developments in Hungary during 1995–97 illustrate one of the most remarkable cases of macroeconomic adjustment in Europe over the last decade. At the end of 1994, macroeconomic conditions in Hungary were worrisome by any standard: the external deficit had exceeded 9 percent of GDP for two years; net external debt had increased rapidly to more than 45 percent of GDP; the deficit of the general government had exceeded 8 percent of GDP; public debt exceeded 85 percent of GDP; and borrowing conditions, for both public and external debt, were deteriorating. Three years later, the external current account deficit had dropped below 3 percent of GDP, reflecting an upsurge in exports, and was financed entirely by foreign direct investment; net external debt in relation to GDP had declined to its lowest level in the 1990s; and major rating agencies had raised their rating of Hungary's external debt to an investment grade.

Hungary's record of external adjustment is even more remarkable compared with the performance of other countries in the region, of which almost all experienced a sizable deterioration in their external accounts during the same period (Figure 2.1). Moreover, the external adjustment in Hungary did not involve a major output loss: while output growth remained well below potential (Chapter VI), it was positive both during 1995 and 1996, and is estimated to have accelerated briskly in 1997 (Table 2.1).

What is behind this turnaround in economic performance? To answer this question, a brief discussion of the factors underlying the 1993–94 crisis is necessary.

Roots of the 1993–94 Crisis

The external and fiscal imbalances that peaked in 1993–94[1] can be traced back to the output shock suffered by the country in the early 1990s as a result of the collapse of the Council for Mutual Economic Assistance (CMEA) trade, the breakdown of key economic relationships and institutions that had prevailed under communism, and the recession in Europe. During 1990–92, output dropped by a cumulative 18 percent and the subsequent recovery, while relatively subdued, quickly ran into a balance of payments constraint. Other transition economies

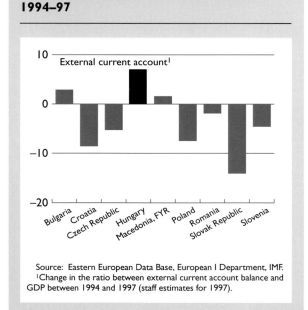

Figure 2.1. Change in External Current Account in Central and Eastern Europe, 1994–97

Source: Eastern European Data Base, European I Department, IMF.
[1]Change in the ratio between external current account balance and GDP between 1994 and 1997 (staff estimates for 1997).

---

[1]Hungary's economic developments through 1994 have also been discussed, from an international perspective, in Boote and Somogyi (1991) and Krueger and Lutz (1995).

Table 2.1. Selected Economic Indicators

	1990	1991	1992	1993	1994	1995	1996	Estimate 1997
Real economy (change in percent)								
Real GDP	−3.5	−11.9	−3.1	−0.6	2.9	1.5	1.3	4.0
Real domestic demand	−3.1	−9.1	−3.6	9.9	2.2	−3.8	−0.8	2.9
Of which: Private consumption	−3.6	−5.6	0.0	1.9	−0.2	−7.1	−3.1	2.4
Gross fixed investment	7.1	−10.4	−2.6	2.0	12.5	−4.3	6.3	11.3
Exports (real)	1.2	−13.9	2.1	−10.1	13.7	13.4	7.4	23.0
Imports (real)[1]	1.8	−6.1	0.2	20.2	8.8	−0.7	5.7	21.5
Average gross wages (industry)	24.9	29.8	26.1	25.8	20.8	21.2	21.5	21.1
CPI (end-year)	34.6	31.0	24.7	21.1	21.2	28.3	19.8	18.4
GDP deflator	25.7	25.4	21.5	21.3	19.5	25.5	20.3	18.0
Employment	...	−3.2	−10.6	−10.2	−5.2	−2.3	−1.8	...
Unemployment rate (end-year, in percent of labor force)	1.9	7.5	12.3	12.1	10.4	10.4	10.5	10.4
Nominal GDP (in billions of forint)[2]	2,282.4	2,521.7	2,970.3	3,581.5	4,405.7	5,614.0	6,845.4	8,400.7
Public finance (percent of GDP)[3]								
Consolidated government balance (excluding privatization receipts)	1.1	−3.3	−7.2	−7.8	−7.1	−6.4	−3.2	−4.6
Primary balance, excluding privatization[4]	6.6	2.6	−1.7	−3.3	−1.3	1.9	4.4	3.8
Public debt (consolidated government)	66.3	73.4	77.6	87.9	85.2	84.3	72.1	63.9
Money (end-of-year, percent change)								
M3	29.6	35.9	27.6	15.3	13.0	20.2	22.1	19.8
Interest rate (90–day treasury bill level, end-year)	33.7	36.6	15.5	26.6	35.6	33.7	23.5	...
Gross national saving[5]	27.6	18.1	15.3	10.6	14.4	20.4	22.4	23.4
Gross investment[5]	25.6	20.6	16.1	20.0	22.2	24.1	24.5	25.4
Balance of payments								
Current account (percent of GDP)[1, 5]	0.4	1.2	0.9	−10.9	−9.7	−5.7	−3.8	−2.7
(In billions of U.S. dollars)	0.1	0.4	0.4	−4.3	−4.1	−2.5	−1.7	−1.2
Reserves in convertible currencies (National valuation of gold, billions of U.S. dollars)	1.2	4.0	4.4	6.7	6.8	12.0	9.8	9.1
(In months of merchandise imports)	2.4	4.8	4.3	7.1	5.3	8.6	5.7	5.4
Gross external debt in convertible currencies (end-year)[6]								
In percent of GDP	64.3	67.1	57.0	63.0	68.1	70.9	61.6	56.2
In billions of U.S. dollars	21.3	22.7	21.4	24.6	28.5	31.7	27.6	25.3
Net external debt in convertible currencies (end-year)[6]								
In percent of GDP	44.5	43.1	35.3	38.3	45.2	37.6	31.8	29.3
In billions of U.S. dollars	15.9	14.6	13.1	14.9	18.9	16.3	14.3	13.2
Exchange rate (annual average)								
Exchange rate regime	*(Crawling peg with respect to a basket of the deutsche mark and U.S. dollar)*							
Nominal effective rate (1990 = 100)	100	88.8	84.9	81.3	72.0	56.1	48.1	41.7
CPI real effective rate (1990 = 100)	100	111.6	120.5	131.3	130.3	125.2	128.0	131.2

Sources: Data provided by the Hungarian authorities; *International Financial Statistics*; and IMF staff estimates.

[1]In 1993, includes imports of military equipment from Russia in lieu of outstanding claims by Hungary.

[2]The official estimates of nominal GDP for years prior to 1995 have been adjusted upward by 0.94 percent to render them consistent with the official data for the following years.

[3]The figures on public finance in this table refer to the "consolidated government" for which a consistent time series exists for the whole period (see Box 5.1 in Chapter V for a definition of consolidated government). Deficit figures for a more comprehensive definition, which includes also the profit position of the central bank and the expenditure of the state privatization agency, are presented in Box 2.1 in this chapter.

[4]Overall balance, excluding net interest expenditure and other debt charges. The figures for 1994–97 also exclude profit transfers from the National Bank of Hungary and transfers to cover National Bank of Hungary losses.

[5]The current account deficit is on a settlements basis and differs from the saving-investment balance, which is on a national accounts basis.

[6]Including intercompany loans.

Box 2.1. A Comprehensive Measure of the Fiscal Policy Stance

To get a comprehensive definition of fiscal policy stance, the deficit figures for the general government (see Chapter V for a definition of the latter) are adjusted here for a number of factors.

		1994	1995	1996	Estimate 1997
		(In billions of forint, unless otherwise indicated)			
(a)	General government deficit (excluding receipts from privatization)	368	373	213	369
(b)	Relevant APV Rt expenditure	8	21	36	80
(c)	Miscellaneous items	0	−20	98	24
(d)	Inflation adjustment	150	283	340	417
(e)	Operational deficit (d-e) (In percent of GDP)	226 (5.1)	91 (1.6)	7 (0.1)	56 (0.7)
(f)	Corresponding primary surplus (In percent of GDP)	−126 (−2.9)	72 (1.3)	240 (3.5)	214 (2.6)

The general government deficit (a) is first adjusted for the component of the expenditure of APV Rt (the agency in charge of privatization) that has a macroeconomic impact (transfers to enterprises, investment expenditure, subsidies) plus the transfers to the general government not formally regarded as privatization receipts under (a). Second, the deficit is adjusted for miscellaneous items (c), the largest of which is the difference between cash and accrual position in the profit and loss accounts of the National Bank of Hungary.[1] Third, the figures are adjusted for the difference between nominal and real interest payments on the consolidated debt of the general government and the central bank (d). This yields the operational deficit (e).

_____

[1]This adjustment is necessary to have a full consolidation of the balance sheet of the two institutions. As the profits of the National Bank of Hungary are transferred to the state budget, and as the budget covers the deficit of the National Bank of Hungary whenever there is a need, in principle the state budget already represents a consolidated balance sheet of the two institutions. However, the profit and loss account of the National Bank of Hungary that is used to compute the transfers to the budget (or the need for transfers from the budget) is compiled on an accrual basis. Thus, to get the consolidated deficit on a cash basis, it is necessary to adjust the government deficit for the difference between cash and accrual position in the National Bank of Hungary profit and loss account. Note that the consolidation between the National Bank of Hungary and the general government is important given the deterioration in the profit and loss of the National Bank of Hungary related to sterilized intervention (Neményi, 1996). It is also important because in 1997, the zero-yield "valuation account"—a credit of the National Bank of Hungary toward the government—was converted into an interest-bearing credit (Chapter IV).

in the region suffered from similar, or larger, output losses, with severe effects on export capacity. In Hungary, however, the effect of the shock on the external balance was exacerbated by the policy attempt to shelter the household sector as much as possible from the effect of the economic crisis (Kornai, 1997). This attempt is apparent in virtually all aspects of macroeconomic policymaking before 1995:

- As the tax base shrank, public expenditure failed to adjust commensurately, and the fiscal balance (excluding privatization receipts) moved from a surplus in 1990 to a large deficit position (Table 2.1 and Box 2.1).

- Reflecting soft budget constraints in public enterprises and generous increases in minimum wages, real wages declined less than output, and income distribution shifted from employers to households (that is, from a high-saving sector to a low-saving sector).

- Monetary policy was relaxed during 1992, with real interest rates remaining negative until the fall of 1993.

- Exchange rate policy was used to contain the increase in the consumer price index (CPI)—and the decline in real disposable income, given the rigidity in nominal wage growth; inflation remained fairly low, compared with other transition economies (Table 2.1), but at the cost of a sizable appreciation of the real exchange rate (Figure 2.2).

The consequences of these policies for the saving-investment balance of the country were harmful. As real private consumption declined by only 1½ percent a year during 1990–94 (against an average output decline of 3½ percent), private saving in percent of GDP edged downward, at the same time that public saving collapsed (Table 2.2). The impact of the fall in domestic saving on the external account was initially cushioned by the fall in enterprise investment. But, as investment recovered in 1993–94, the current account imbalance widened to levels that were unsustainable, despite comparatively large nondebt capital inflows (foreign direct investment (FDI); Table 2.3).

The dramatic worsening of the current account highlighted a long-standing weakness of the Hungarian economy: its high external debt ratio. Hungary's external debt had increased rapidly during the 1970s and the 1980s. Despite a sizable drop in the early 1990s (reflecting a broadly balanced current account position and increasingly inward FDI, including privatization receipts), net external debt stood at about 35 percent of GDP at the end of 1992 (Table 2.3) and had climbed to 45 percent of GDP by the end of 1994 (a high level by international standards).

Against this gloomy macroeconomic background, some structural developments—which were to prove important to the subsequent recovery—had taken place. By the end of the 1980s, the price system had been liberalized to a large extent, with regulated prices accounting for only about 20 percent of the CPI basket in 1989. This is a key difference with respect to other transition economies—a difference that helps to explain why the transition in Hungary was not accompanied by a major inflationary outburst (Chapter VII). Moreover, the tax system was reformed during 1988–90 with the introduction of the value-added tax (VAT), personal income tax, and a new enterprise profit tax (Boote and Somogyi, 1991). A two-tier banking system was introduced in 1987 (National Bank of Hungary, 1994). Finally, important trade liberalization measures had been implemented by the beginning of the 1990s (Chapter IX). The most significant areas of progress during the first half of the 1990s were:

- the enactment in January 1992 of a bankruptcy law; this law, while excessively restrictive (Chapter VI), led to the rapid elimination of a large number of loss-making public enterprises, releasing resources to other sectors of the economy;

- the enactment in 1991–92 of modern commercial banking and accounting laws, which forced banks to provision against bad loans (thus highlighting the need for their further restructuring) and contributed to the gradual tightening of the budget constraint on enterprises; and

- the surge of FDI, partly as a result of the privatization process (Chapter VIII) and incentives (including tax incentives) to the establishment of joint ventures; by the end of 1994 and since 1989, cumulative FDI in Hungary equaled the sum of investment in all other transition economies in eastern Europe, central Europe, and Estonia, Latvia, and Lithuania (the Baltic countries).

These steps helped to establish a basis for a supply response, particularly in the export sector. Nevertheless, in 1993–94, the reform process slowed down and eventually stalled, particularly in the fiscal area (Chapters V, VI, and VIII).

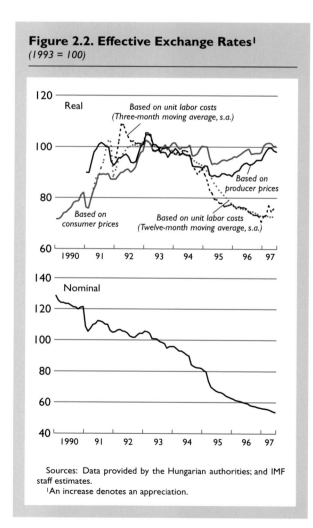

Figure 2.2. Effective Exchange Rates[1]
(1993 = 100)

Sources: Data provided by the Hungarian authorities; and IMF staff estimates.
[1]An increase denotes an appreciation.

Table 2.2. Sectoral Saving and Investment Balances[1]
(In percent of GDP)

	1990	1991	1992	1993	1994	1995	1996
Gross domestic saving	27.6	18.1	15.3	10.6	14.4	20.4	22.4
Government[2]	3.8	1.8	0.5	−1.0	−1.5	−0.8	1.2
Nongovernment	23.8	16.3	14.8	11.6	15.9	21.1	21.2
Gross investment[3]	25.6	20.6	16.1	20.0	22.2	24.1	24.5
Government[2]	4.3	5.0	7.4	6.6	6.9	5.2	4.6
Nongovernment	21.3	15.5	8.6	13.3	15.3	19.0	19.9
Nonfinancial balance	2.0	−2.4	−0.8	−9.3	−7.8	−3.7	−2.1
Government	−0.5	−3.3	−7.0	−7.5	−8.4	−6.0	−3.4
Nongovernment	2.5	0.9	6.2	−1.9	0.6	2.3	1.3

Sources: Central Statistical Office; and Ministry of Finance.
[1]Data based on the new System of National Accounts; staff estimates based on the old national accounts for 1990.
[2]Excludes in 1993 imports of military equipment from Russia in lieu of outstanding claims by Hungary.
[3]Gross investment includes net capital transfers to other domestic sectors.

Economic Goals and Policy Strategy During 1995–97

The adjustment program initiated by the authorities in March 1995 had a clear and immediate objective: to bring the external deficit down to a manageable level, so as to avert the risk of an external crisis. But the overall strategy had more wide-ranging ambitions. The authorities intended to prime an export-led growth process capable of raising the growth rate of the economy to its potential. Achieving these goals required reversing some of the phenomena that had characterized the early 1990s: the profit share in income distribution had to be reversed to contain consumption and stimulate investment; the absorption of saving by the public sector had to be reduced drastically; and external competitiveness had to be restored to stimulate export growth. Reducing inflation (which had lingered in the 20–30 percent range during the 1990s) was not regarded as an immediate priority. On the contrary, it was recognized that a price hike was inevitable and was indeed instrumental in redressing the real imbalances that had developed in the previous year (particularly in income distribution; see below). However, the program aimed to ensure that the price acceleration would be temporary, and that the basis would be laid for a reduction in inflation to single digits in the medium term.

The strategy to achieve these objectives had a macroeconomic component and a structural component. The macroeconomic component had strong orthodox features (the up-front fiscal adjustment and depreciation), coupled with some heterodox features (the use of inflation to correct income distribution in the presence of nominal wage rigidity and the at-tempt to shield domestic monetary policy from external pressures through sterilized intervention). The structural component centered on the revival of the privatization process (to reduce external debt and increase efficiency), the downsizing of the public sector, the increased opening of the economy to foreign trade, and the long-term reform of public finances.

The Macroeconomic Component

A sharp, up-front, fiscal adjustment was inevitable. The fiscal imbalance was not sustainable, as it would have led to a steady increase in the public debt-to-GDP ratio (Chapter IV). But adjustment had to go beyond the mere restoration of fiscal solvency. There was a need to raise domestic saving to reduce the external deficit and finance the expected increase in private investment. The March 1995 adjustment package included several permanent measures (cuts in transfers to households, a reduction in the number of state employees, and a broadening of the social security contribution base), together with the temporary introduction of an 8 percent import surcharge on consumer goods, with an expected annual yield of about 1 percent of GDP (Chapter V). Moreover, the government decided to freeze other expenditures in nominal terms, with the result that the acceleration of inflation (see below) involved a real expenditure cut with respect to the projections underlying the 1995 budget.

The extent of the fiscal adjustment implemented in 1995 can be better appreciated by focusing on a comprehensive definition of the public sector, which includes the National Bank of Hungary (see Box 2.1) and by adjusting the figures for inflation. In-

Table 2.3. Balance of Payments in Convertible Currencies
(In millions of U.S. dollars, unless otherwise specified)

	1990	1991	1992	1993	1994	1995	1996	Estimate 1997
Current account	127	267	325	–3,457	–3,915	–2,480	–1,678	–1,200
Trade balance	348	189	–48	–3,247	–3,634	–2,443	–2,645	–1,800
Exports	6,346	9,258	10,028	8,094	7,614	12,810	14,183	18,800
Imports	5,998	–9,069	–10,076	–11,341	–11,248	–15,253	–16,828	–20,600
Services (net)	–948	–783	–486	–942	–1,189	–1,164	45	–200
Interest income (net)[1]	–1,414	–1,331	–1,216	–1,131	–1,287	–1,599	–1,178	–1,100
Travel (net)	345	560	590	441	504	658	1,288	1,500
Other (net)	121	–12	140	–252	–406	–223	–65	–600
Unrequited transfers	727	861	859	732	908	1,127	922	0.8
Capital account	–538	1,652	444	6,065	3,418	7,805	221	...
Of which: Private (net; including net errors and omissions)	...	...	...	...	...	340	1,598	...
Medium-term liabilities	88	867	–886	3,039	1,326	1,866	–3,008	...
Of which: National Bank of Hungary	...	...	...	...	...	...	–774	...
Foreign direct investment (net)[1]	311	1,459	1,471	2,329	1,097	4,410	1,986	2,000
Of which: Privatization receipts	...	...	...	...	...	3,025	578	600
Intercompany loans	...	...	...	...	...	...	196	...
Other	–937	–674	–141	697	995	1,529	1,243	...
Of which: Net errors and omissions	...	...	...	...	189	1,225	1,864	...
Overall balance	–1,411	1,919	769	2,607	–497	5,325	–1,457	...
Memorandum items:								
Current account (percent of GDP)	0.4	1.2	0.9	–10.9	–9.7	–5.7	–3.8	–2.7
Gross reserves[2]	1,160	4,017	4,380	6,736	6,769	12,010	9,751	9,100
(In months of imports)	2.4	4.8	4.3	7.1	5.3	8.6	5.7	5.4
Convertible gross external debt[3]	21,270	22,658	21,438	24,560	28,522	31,660	27,646	25,300
(In percent of GDP)	64.3	67.1	57.0	63.0	68.1	70.9	61.6	56.2
Net external debt[3]	15,938	14,555	13,052	14,927	18,937	16,336	14,258	13,200
(In percent of GDP)	48.2	43.1	35.3	38.3	45.2	37.6	31.8	29.3

Sources: Hungarian authorities; and IMF staff estimates.
[1]Excludes reinvested profits.
[2]At current exchange rate.
[3]Includes intercompany loans.

deed, in a year in which inflation was rapidly rising, the nominal deficit was boosted by the increase in nominal interest payments necessary to compensate holders of government paper for the erosion in the real value of principal. However, the operational deficit (that is, the deficit adjusted for the difference between nominal and real interest payments) fell by more than 3½ percentage points, while the primary balance improved by almost 4¼ percentage points.

Fiscal adjustment continued in 1996 and 1997, with the main goal of consolidating the results achieved, rather than of implementing a further major fiscal tightening. The fiscal stance was tightened again in 1996, but it was relaxed somewhat in the subsequent year. Altogether, in 1997, the primary balance had strengthened by 1¼ percentage points of GDP with respect to 1995, while the overall oper-

ational deficit had declined by almost 1 percentage point of GDP (Box 2.1).[2] In addition to a further cut

[2]Note that, in the definition reported in Table 2.1, the adjustment in the primary balance between 1995 and 1997 was larger. The figure reported in the text refers to the definition used in Box 2.1, which is more significant from a macroeconomic standpoint. Also note that the fiscal tightening between 1995 and 1996, and the corresponding relaxation between 1996 and 1997, was larger than intended, as the 1996 deficit turned out to be lower than budgeted by about ½ percent of GDP. Moreover, because of the lengthening in the maturity of government securities in 1996, the deficit on an accrual basis in 1996 was larger than the deficit on a cash basis. Finally, the larger increase in the overall deficit in 1997 as measured in Table 2.1, with respect to the increase in the operational deficit in Box 2.1, is due to the increase in interest payments on forint liabilities issued by the government and the National Bank of Hungary as a result of intense sterilization operations (see below). The inflation-related component of these interest payments does not appear in the definition of operational deficit.

in the operational deficit, fiscal policy in 1996–97 achieved two main goals. First, some of the temporary measures that were part of the March 1995 package (including the import surcharge) were replaced by lasting measures. Second, downsizing of the public budget continued, as highlighted by further sizable declines in the public revenues and expenditures ratios, with the effect of stimulating private sector growth.[3]

The choice of the exchange rate policy was dictated by the need to recover the competitiveness lost during the first half of the 1990s, and to provide a nominal anchor to make sure that the inevitable price acceleration was only temporary. The forint was devalued by 9 percent on March 13, 1995, and at the same time, a preannounced crawling exchange rate band was introduced, thus abandoning the policy of discretionary revisions of the parities that had characterized the previous period. The band introduced was relatively narrow (∓ 2.25 percent), so as to provide a clear indication of the authorities' intentions. The rate of crawl was initially sizable (1.9 percent a month through June 30, 1995), so as to guarantee a further improvement in competitiveness, but was then gradually reduced.[4]

Why was the exchange rate preferred to other nominal anchors, and what were the implications of such a choice? In many respects, the choice of the exchange rate as the nominal anchor was inevitable. Traditionally, the exchange rate in Hungary, as in many other small, open economies, has been highly visible. As such, it represents an important focus for the formation of the private sector's expectations. Moreover, the natural alternative, targeting some monetary aggregate, was made difficult by the instability of money demand, which was related to wide-ranging structural changes in the Hungarian financial and payments system (Box 2.2). The choice of the exchange rate as the nominal anchor had, however, an important consequence for the shape of economic policies during 1995–97. Given that the primary focus of the adjustment program was external, the rate of crawl could hardly be used aggressively to disinflate the economy: the possibility of faster disinflation was regarded as a poor compensation for the external account risks arising from tighter exchange rate policies. Thus, it is not surprising that the reduction in the rate of crawl between the second half of 1995 and the second half of 1997 was rather modest.

As mentioned, the adjustment program also had important heterodox features. The first relates to the mechanism through which the needed redistribution of income from employees to employers was brought about. Between the end of 1994 and the middle of 1995, inflation increased from about 21 percent to more than 32 percent, reflecting sharp adjustments in administered prices (particularly in the energy sector) and the depreciation of the forint. This inflationary outburst was to a large extent unexpected and had not been incorporated in the wage agreements for 1995, most of which had been concluded before the March stabilization program was announced. The main effort required was to make sure that the agreed wage increases were not revised on account of higher inflation. To this end, the authorities primarily used their influence over wage developments in the public sector and the public enterprise sector. In the public sector, the decision not to revise the budgetary outlays for 1995 discouraged decentralized spending units from granting wages in excess of those provided for in the budget. As to the public enterprise sector, still sizable at that time, instructions were issued to avoid a wage acceleration. There was no formal agreement with trade unions, though. The fact that the authorities' tough wage policy was accepted without disruption of work activity shows the unions' sense of responsibility and the fact that an adjustment in real wages was regarded as inevitable.[5] Incomes policy agreements were instead reached in 1996 and in 1997 in the context of the Interest Reconciliation Council (IRC).[6] In 1996, the IRC recommended an average increase in gross wages of 19½ percent, with a range of 13–24 percent to allow for different productivity growth across sectors. The agreement assumed an inflation rate of 18 percent. In the event, inflation was much higher (see below), while gross wage growth in the public sector (although not in the private sector) increased by less than recommended. Again, this contributed to the strengthening of fiscal accounts. The overshooting of inflation in 1995–96, however,

---

[3]See Chapter V for a detailed discussion of the changes in the level and structure of public expenditure and revenues during 1995–97.

[4]The rate of crawl was 1.3 percent a month in the second half of 1995; 1.2 percent a month during January 1996–March 1997; and 1.1 percent a month from April 1997 until mid-August 1997, when it was lowered to 1 percent. Through December 1996, the forint was pegged to a basket of the European currency unit (ECU) (70 percent) and the U.S. dollar (30 percent). As of January 1997, the ECU was replaced by the deutsche mark.

[5]Other factors were also important. In Hungary, the role of trade unions in the emerging private sector branches (particularly in multinational corporations) has been modest (Chapter X). In these branches, wage increases are decided at the beginning of the year, often without consultation with the trade unions. Wages are not revised until the following year. This facilitated the erosion of real wages in the second half of 1995.

[6]The IRC is a tripartite institution comprising representatives of trade unions, the government, and some employers' associations. It issues recommendations for wage increases in the private sector, which are not binding.

Box 2.2.   How Stable Is Money Demand?

The decision to adopt an exchange rate rule in March 1995 rather than to target some monetary aggregate was based in part on the perceived difficulty of reliably forecasting money demand during a period of heightened macroeconomic uncertainty and structural transformation, in addition to the absence of a timely and accurate indicator of real economic activity.

Monetary developments since then have tended to support that decision. While the real value of M3 (currency, bank deposits, and bank-issued financial securities) remained relatively constant during 1992–94, real M3 declined sharply (by 17 percent) between the end of 1994 and early 1996, before recovering somewhat since then (see figure below). This dramatic reduction in financial intermediation is also apparent in each of the major components of M3. While this is not evidence of instability per se, the evidence lies in the fact that the decline in the monetary aggregate is poorly correlated with the level of real activity and interest rates. As a consequence, had a monetary target based on historical behavior been adopted during this period, the monetary stance would have been different than intended by the authorities.

The implications of the instability in money demand for monetary targeting can be seen using a multivariate error correction model (VECM) of the form:

$$\Delta Z_t = \Gamma_1 \Delta Z_{t-1} + \ldots + \Gamma_k \Delta Z_{t-k+1} + \Pi Z_{t-1} + \mu_t \qquad (1)$$

where Z is a vector of the variables $\log(M3adj)$, $\log(prod)$, pi, Rd^L, $Rtb3comp$; $\log(M3adj)$ is the natural log of real M3, adjusted for interest accrued but not yet paid on deposits; $\log(prod)$ is the natural log of the volume of industrial production; pi is the 12-month inflation rate; Rd^L is the interest rate on deposits held for more than 12 months; $Rtb3comp$ is the compound interest yield on 3-month treasury bills; and Δ indicates the first difference of the variable. An intercept and a

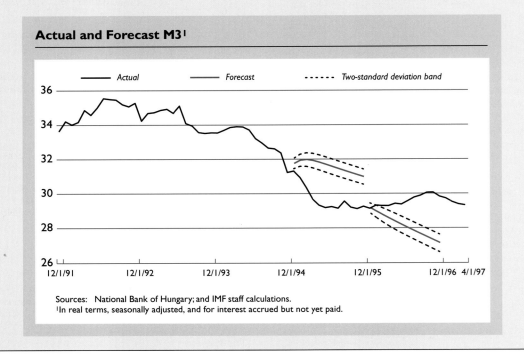

Actual and Forecast M3[1]

Sources: National Bank of Hungary; and IMF staff calculations.
[1]In real terms, seasonally adjusted, and for interest accrued but not yet paid.

made the 1997 wage agreement more difficult, and led authorities to announce a relatively unambitious inflation target for that year (see below).

The second heterodox aspect of the adjustment program was related to monetary policy. Over 1995–97, monetary policy strove to keep forint interest rates shielded from external pressures through sterilized intervention. The Hungarian experience shows that, under certain conditions, it is possible to maintain some monetary independence for a fairly long period of time even in the presence of a narrow exchange rate band.[7] During 1995–97, the interest rate differential with the deutsche mark, adjusted for the announced rate of depreciation, al-

---

[7]Moreover, for most of 1995–97, the forint remained close to the more appreciated margin of the band, so that the risk of a depreciation within the band may have appeared limited.

linear time trend are included in the long-run model. All variables are seasonally adjusted.

Based on the data available through the time, the new exchange regime was introduced (December 1991 to December 1994) and Johansen's methodology, a cointegrating relationship is found to exist between M3, industrial production, interest rates, and inflation:[1]

$$L(M3adj) = \alpha + 0.31\,L(prod) + 0.0015\,Rd^L \\ - 0.0026\,Rtb3comp - 0.0067\,pi \\ - 0.0051\,Trend \qquad (2)$$

These results imply that a 1 percentage point increase in industrial production raises M3 by 0.3 percentage point; an increase in the interest rate on deposits increases M3, while an increase in inflation (which represents a cost of holding currency) and in the yield paid on treasury bills (which are a substitute for M3) lower M3. However, these relative price effects are found to be quite small, in line with the empirical findings of other researchers. Since the estimation period covers the initial period of banking sector disintermediation, money demand is found to have a negative trend component.

Using the estimates from the VECM formulation, it is possible to forecast the level of money demand during 1995. Had a monetary rule been pursued during this period, such forecasts would have been used to establish monetary targets under the program. One can see from the figure that the model performs poorly out of sample, providing forecasts of M3 during 1995 well above the actual level.[2] The actual level of M3 is outside the two-standard deviation band around the forecast throughout the projection period. This would suggest that, had Hungary followed a monetary target at that time, financial policies would have been excessively lax.

The poor predictive power of the money demand model can be related to the difficulty of capturing the process of financial disintermediation through the inclusion in the equation of trend variables. In particular, a number of factors may have accelerated the financial disintermediation process in 1995. The increased presence of foreign banks in the domestic banking system led to substantial modernization of banking and payments technologies. These innovations included the introduction of (1) automated teller machines (ATMs) (which enabled Hungarians to re-

duce their average holdings of currency by lowering the transaction costs associated with withdrawal); (2) credit cards (which may have reduced households' average deposit balances since purchases no longer needed to be financed by drawing down accumulated deposits); and (3) a more efficient interbank clearance system (which served to lower the demand for transaction money balances by limiting the time needed to effect payments, thereby reducing the amount of money in transit). Moreover, a wider range of nonbank savings instruments became available—and more accessible—during this period, including inflation-indexed government bonds, investment and pension funds, and equities.

One would hope that, by adding additional information, the predictive power of the model would improve. Unfortunately, based on a reestimation of the model through December 1995,[3] actual money demand is substantially more than 2 standard deviations *above* the forecast level throughout all but the first quarter of 1996. This underestimation may be partially related to the omission of some relevant variables from the model.[4] More fundamentally, it reflects the difficulty of predicting the effect of financial innovation and disintermediation through a trend component.

The relative constancy of real M3 in 1996 following several years of trend decline suggests that forecasting could become more reliable in the future.

This box was prepared by Rachel van Elkan.

[1]Two cointegrating vectors were found to be present. On the basis of theoretical priors regarding the signs and magnitudes of the elements of the vectors, one eigenvector was rejected.

[2]The inclusion of squared and cubic trend terms did not improve the forecasting performance of the model.

[3]The long-run cointegrating relationship for the period 1992:1 to 1995:12 is:

$$L(M3adj) = \alpha + 0.31\,L(prod) + 0.0026\,Rd^L \\ - 0.0035\,Rtb3comp - 0.0061\,pi \\ - 0.0044\,Trend.$$

[4]The cost of reserve requirements declined in 1996 (Chapter XI); insofar as this decline led to a spread between lending rates and treasury bill rates (and assuming that money demand is affected negatively by lending rates), the omission from equation (1) of the lending rate may explain an underprediction in 1996.

---

ways remained positive, initially at about 5–10 percentage points, and after the spring of 1996 in the 3–4 percentage point range (Figure 2.3). Taking into account domestic inflation, this was enough to keep real interest rates on government paper positive (at about 1–2 percent using ex post inflation rates—Figure 2.3—and probably higher using expected inflation rates). This policy succeeded for several reasons. First, constraints on capital move-

ments, both inward and outward, have been in place, and were more stringent for short-term investment (Chapter XII). Although they may have been partially circumvented (as suggested by sizable errors and omissions in the balance of payments), they nevertheless helped to shield domestic monetary policy. Second, the limited liquidity of Hungarian financial assets reduced the attractiveness of speculative investment for foreigners, al-

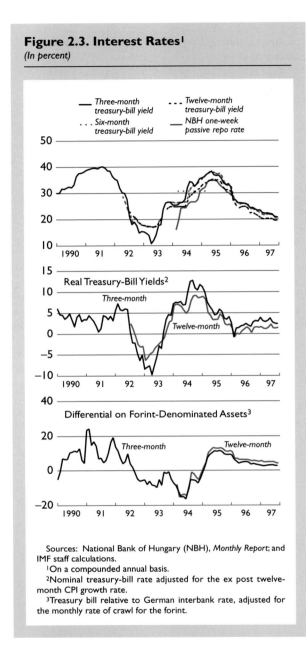

Figure 2.3. Interest Rates[1]
(In percent)

Sources: National Bank of Hungary (NBH), *Monthly Report*; and IMF staff calculations.

[1]On a compounded annual basis.

[2]Nominal treasury-bill rate adjusted for the ex post twelve-month CPI growth rate.

[3]Treasury bill relative to German interbank rate, adjusted for the monthly rate of crawl for the forint.

repayment of external debt, with an implicit high yield, thus reducing the cost of sterilized intervention commensurately.[9] Nevertheless, the extent of the foreign exchange intervention was impressive. It amounted to 80 percent of base money in 1995, and to a still sizable estimated 50 percent in 1997.

The Structural Component

The goals of the structural adjustment program in 1995–97 were to reduce Hungary's external debt through privatization receipts from abroad, strengthen the supply response of the system, and consolidate the progress made in the fiscal balances.

A key step was the revival of the privatization process, which had stalled in 1994 (Chapter VIII). Privatization receipts during 1995–97 amounted to a cumulative 12 percentage points of GDP (against 8 percentage points in the preceding five years), more than 80 percent of which came from abroad. This had three beneficial effects on the economy. First, it facilitated the increase in productivity needed to sustain output growth in the medium term as foreign ownership injected fresh capital and know-how. Second, it contributed critically to the decline in public and external debt ratios, reducing the country's exposure to external shocks. Third, it involved sizable savings for both the fiscal deficit and the external current account.[10]

Another important step was the further relaxation of constraints on external transactions. Important measures in the liberalization of capital transactions were undertaken, partly reflecting the requirements for acceding to the OECD (Chapter XII). The trade liberalization process was also continued (Chapter IX). There was a further relaxation of the remaining import quotas (which, already in 1994, covered a relatively limited number of goods). The effective tariff rate (i.e., the ratio between tariff and fees revenues and the total import value) did increase in 1995, reflecting the above-mentioned import surcharge, but fell rapidly in the following two years as the import surcharge faded away and underlying tariffs and fees were reduced or removed in line with Hungary's international commitments. Indeed, the effective tariff rate in 1998 is expected to be one-third of its 1994 level.

Fiscal reform focused on the reduction in the overall size of the public sector and on social security reform. While official data tend to overstate the

though probably not for residents.[8] Third, the cost of sterilized intervention was lowered in Hungary by the fact that, in early 1995, the stock of external debt issued at high spreads was quite large: foreign exchange reserves purchased by the National Bank of Hungary in the market could be used for early

---

[8]A large share of foreign exchange market intervention reflected reverse currency substitution (in particular, domestic banks converting into forint their large stock of foreign exchange reserves deposited at the central bank).

---

[9]Refinancing the whole stock of old debt through new borrowing would have been problematic (keeping gross borrowing low facilitated the decline in the spread). In any case, the spread on new issues declined only gradually from high levels in early 1995.

[10]As the average interest rate paid on external debt by Hungary at the end of 1994 was fairly large, the cumulative privatization of 1995–97 resulted in annual savings of about ¾ percent of GDP for the external current account and the public sector budget.

magnitude of the phenomenon (Chapter V), primary revenues and expenditure ratios dropped by about 10–15 percentage points of GDP between 1994 and 1997 (albeit from high levels). The revenue drop reflected sizable cuts in enterprise taxes and trade tariffs (but households taxes were also lowered). It may also have been affected by increased tax erosion and evasion, although, in the same period, several measures were undertaken to strengthen tax administration. On the expenditure side, in March 1997, public employment stood at about 11 percent below its level of three years before. Outlays for subsidies, pensions, and investment also declined in relation to GDP. Important structural reforms—with less immediate effects on the deficit but crucial for the medium- to long-term evolution of public finances—were also undertaken in the social security area. The most important reform was the pension reform: enacted in two steps—in 1996 and 1997—it involved an increase in pension age, penalties for early retirement, a revision in the pension indexation mechanism, and the introduction of a fully funded component of the pension system, aimed at providing about 25–30 percent of pension revenues in the long run. Parliament also approved a resolution assigning to the government the mandate to reform the disability pension system, but a new law in this area is not expected until after the May 1998 elections.[11] Measures were also introduced to rationalize the health system (reductions in pharmaceutical subsidies, and steps to reduce unused hospital capacity). However, the reform laws enacted in 1997, while providing a useful streamlining of existing legislation, fell short of what was needed to give the health system sounder and more efficient foundations (Chapter V).

Results of the Adjustment Program

External Accounts

During 1995–97, the performance of the Hungarian economy improved in almost all respects. The most impressive result of the program was the dramatic turnaround in the external accounts, which is illustrated by two key statistics: the external current account deficit fell from 9½ percent of GDP in 1994 to a projected 2¾ percent of GDP in 1997; and net external debt was lowered from more than 45 percent of GDP to less than 30 percent of GDP.[12]

This turnaround benefited from favorable external conditions (the growth rate of imports of Hungary's partner countries was 7 percent in 1995–97, against 4½ percent during the first half of the 1990s), but should be credited primarily to the policies implemented by the authorities.

To clarify the link between economic policies and external developments, it is useful to break down the external current account into an interest component and a noninterest component. As shown in Figure 2.4, the improvement in the noninterest component is closely correlated with the improvement in the fiscal balance. Of course, the adjustment also required a corresponding adjustment in the real exchange rate, which was overvalued at the end of 1994. However, after the initial adjustment in 1995, the CPI-based real exchange rate gradually recovered and eventually exceeded its end-1994 value. On the other hand, the depreciation of the unit-labor-cost-based real exchange rate persisted (and was about 20 percent; Figure 2.2). The different behavior of the two real exchange rates reflects a number of factors, including increasing profit margin and faster productivity growth in the tradable vis-à-vis the nontradable sector, strengthened by the fact that adherence to the incomes policy guidelines proved to be somewhat stricter in the tradable sector, possibly reflecting the discipline imposed by the exchange rate peg. The improved competitiveness of Hungarian exports is evidenced by the steep increase in the dollar receipts for ex-

---

[11]The disability pension system is poorly targeted. As a result, people of working age receiving disability pensions represented almost 9 percent of the workforce in 1997.

[12]The reduction is even larger excluding intracompany loans, which increased rapidly in 1995–97.

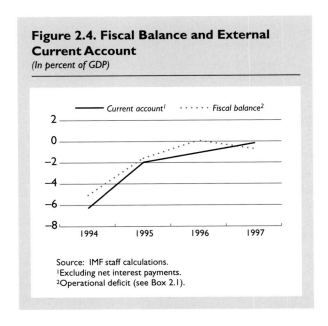

Figure 2.4. Fiscal Balance and External Current Account
(In percent of GDP)

Source: IMF staff calculations.
[1]Excluding net interest payments.
[2]Operational deficit (see Box 2.1).

Figure 2.5. External Current Account and Trade Balance
(Three-month moving average, millions of U.S. dollars)

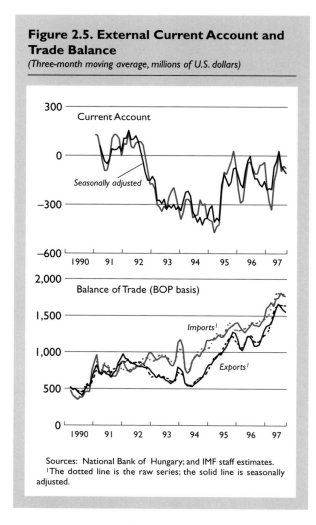

Sources: National Bank of Hungary; and IMF staff estimates.
[1]The dotted line is the raw series; the solid line is seasonally adjusted.

Table 2.4. Factors Underlying the Change in Net External Debt, 1995–97
(In billions of U.S. dollars)

Change in net external debt[1]	−5.7
Current account deficit	5.4
Foreign direct investment (excluding privatization receipts and intercompany loans)	−3.7
Privatization receipts	−4.2
Errors and omissions in the balance of payments	−3.6
Other[2]	0.3

[1]Including intercompany loans.
[2]Including changes in cross exchange rates.

ports, which outstripped the sharp rise in imports (Figure 2.5).[13]

The improvement in the current account also reflected a sizable decline in the burden of net interest payments, which dropped by 1¼ percentage points of GDP between 1995 and 1997.[14] This drop was due to two factors: the decline in the stock of net ex-

ternal debt and the authorities' active policy of refinancing high interest loans undertaken before 1995 with lower interest loans, as the risk premium on Hungarian government debt declined sharply.

The reduction in the current account deficit and the increased privatization receipts from abroad were, of course, key factors behind the drop in net external debt. Other factors were at play, some of which may be related more to the overall improvement of Hungary's economic conditions than to specific policy measures undertaken by the authorities. Table 2.4 provides a breakdown of the factors behind the decline in net external debt. The table highlights the importance of FDI and, in particular, of privatization receipts. It also shows that a large component of the decline in net external debt (about $3.5 billion out of an overall decline of about $5¾ billion) cannot be identified precisely, as it corresponds to the errors and omissions in the balance of payments. This item is likely to include both current account transactions (which would give rise to a genuine decline in net external debt) and capital account transactions (which would largely be matched by unrecorded debt components). It is also possible that the errors and omissions item hides, as a result of a "confidence effect" in the forint, the surfacing of unrecorded financial assets held abroad illegally by residents. It is impossible to quantify the relative size of these components, particularly during a period in which there was a significant improvement in both recorded current account and capital account transactions.

Output Growth, Aggregate Demand Composition, and Unemployment

A slowing down of economic activity was regarded as the inevitable by-product of the adjust-

---

[13]The figure, as well as the data in Table 2.1, may overstate the actual increase in external trade. Export receipts in 1994 may have been artificially depressed by hidden capital outflows. Moreover, anecdotal evidence indicates that imports for reexport increased rapidly during 1995–96. The further sharp increases in imports and exports recorded in early 1997 may also be due to changes in the recording of some imports for reexport from a net basis to a gross basis.

[14]The comparison with 1995 is more significant than that with 1994 because the increase in interest rates on Hungarian debt observed in 1994 was reflected in interest payments only in 1995. Moreover, to a large extent, the interest savings related to privatization receipts were not felt until 1996, as privatization receipts in 1995 were concentrated in December.

ment program. On average during the 1990s, and even after the initial output shock had been absorbed, output growth in Hungary remained well below its potential (Chapter VI). Nevertheless, the output acceleration of 1994 (Table 2.1) was clearly not sustainable, as it relied excessively on domestic demand and soon clashed against the external constraint. The program's envisaged shift of resources toward the external sector was accompanied by a deceleration of growth in 1995–96. However, it is remarkable that, despite the magnitude of the required external adjustment, output growth remained positive in both 1995 and 1996, and accelerated briskly in 1997 (Table 2.1 and Figure 2.6). This result owes much to the structural changes that had already taken place in the first half of the 1990s. These changes allowed the export sector to react promptly to the macroeconomic stimuli coming from economic policies.

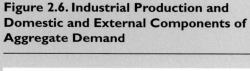

Figure 2.6. Industrial Production and Domestic and External Components of Aggregate Demand

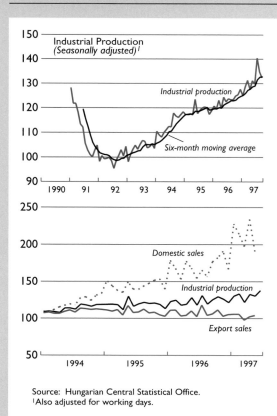

Source: Hungarian Central Statistical Office.
[1] Also adjusted for working days.

The extent of the adjustment of aggregate demand from internal and external components is illustrated by Figure 2.6 (lower panel) and Figure 6.1 in Chapter VI. The contribution of external transactions to growth turned from minus 5 percentage points in the average of 1993–94 to plus 3½ percentage points in 1995–96. This exceeded the negative contribution that was coming from domestic consumption and investment. The decline in consumption was expected and was indeed an integral part of the adjustment process. The adjustment was painful: net real wages dropped by a cumulative 16½ percent in 1995–96 (Figure 2.7), and private consumption dropped by 10 percent. By 1997, however, both real wages and private consumption had begun to recover. The response of fixed investment was initially lukewarm: investment accelerated only in the second quarter of 1996. This delayed recovery is understandable. Even though enterprises' internal financial sources improved rapidly in 1995, it stands to reason that enterprises initially took a wait-and-see attitude, given the uncertainty about the success of the stabilization, before launching new investment projects, particularly in domestically oriented activities (FDI, even excluding privatization, remained high throughout the period). Moreover, housing investment was constrained by the squeeze in households' cash flow and cuts in housing subsidies.

During the last three years, the unemployment rate has remained broadly constant at about 10–11 percent, and has failed to decline even during the most recent recovery (Figure 2.8). While in all countries employment lags behind output, a decisive increase in employment may require structural measures—such as a further reduction in labor taxes and a reform of the income support schemes that would discourage the active search for jobs (see Chapter X).

Inflation

As argued above, the main target of the authorities' 1995–97 adjustment program was external. The establishment of a crawling exchange rate regime aimed at avoiding a permanent acceleration of inflation, which indeed was initially expected to come down quite rapidly in 1996 and 1997. In the event, however, progress on the inflation front was more limited than initially envisaged (Table 2.5 and Figure 2.9): the 12-month inflation rate was 18.4 percent in December 1997, one of the lowest levels in the 1990s, but still not too far from the range in which inflation had remained in 1993–94.

The resiliency of inflation in 1996–97 reflects in part the authorities' priorities (the need to avoid excessive risks to the external sector), and in part objective factors raising the cost of disinflation (see Chapter VII). These difficulties included sticky in-

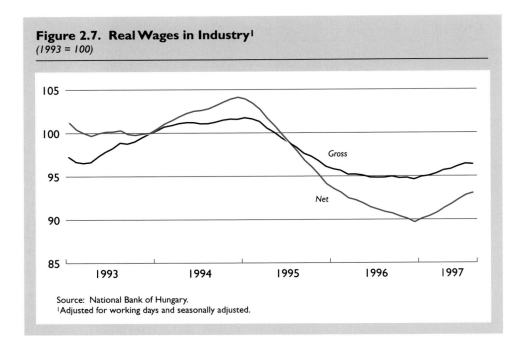

Figure 2.7. Real Wages in Industry[1]
(1993 = 100)

Source: National Bank of Hungary.
[1]Adjusted for working days and seasonally adjusted.

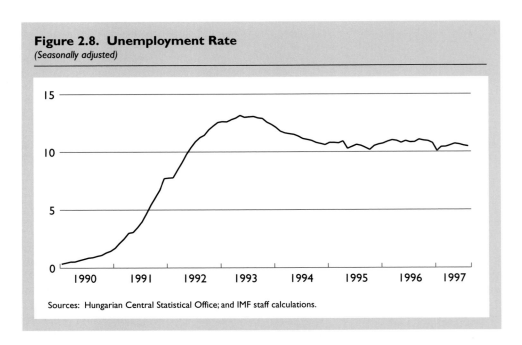

Figure 2.8. Unemployment Rate
(Seasonally adjusted)

Sources: Hungarian Central Statistical Office; and IMF staff calculations.

flation expectations, after years of moderate but steady inflation—a difficulty that had been exacerbated by the peak in inflation in 1995; the still limited credibility of the newly established monetary framework; and continued pressure on prices arising from the transition process (in particular, the needed changes in administered prices). These difficulties are apparent in 1996, a key period, as price developments that year also explain the authorities' decision to revise the inflation target upward for 1997.

The authorities' target for 1996 was ambitious: inflation was expected to fall by more than 10 per-

Table 2.5. Consumer Price Index Inflation Targets and Outcomes

	Sept. 1994	March 1995	Original[1]	Revised[2]	Original[1]	Revised[2]
		1995		1996		1997
Average inflation						
Target	22¾	26–27	18	23½	13	18
Actual		28¼		23½		18¼

[1]Targets set in December 1995, as part of the IMF-supported adjustment program.
[2]Revised in June 1996.

Figure 2.9. CPI Inflation
(Twelve-month growth rate)

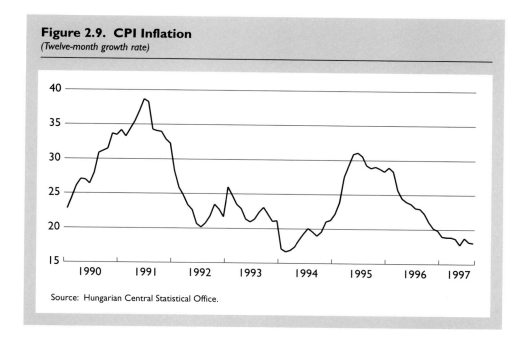

Source: Hungarian Central Statistical Office.

centage points with respect to 1995. In the event, inflation did drop fairly rapidly, but was about 5½ percentage points above target. This overshooting was due primarily to two factors: first, the limited credibility of the anti-inflationary program and the related failure of the incomes policy guidelines to keep gross wages in line with the target, which was more evident in the private nonmanufacturing sector; and, second, further large increases in administered prices, whose extent had initially been underestimated.[15] By the spring of 1996, it had become apparent that inflation would exceed the target and the authorities were faced with the difficult choice of revising the target or tightening policies (including exchange rate policy). As the latter option would have involved significant risks for output and external developments, the inflation target was revised for both 1996 and 1997. A key factor in this decision was the expected difficulty of reaching an incomes policy agreement with trade unions for 1997 based on low nominal wage increases after the overshooting of inflation in both 1995 and 1996.[16] The decision resulted in a limited decline in inflation through 1997. However, it had a positive effect: with inflation developments in 1997 broadly

[15]Initially, it had been expected that the increase in administered prices would raise the CPI by about 2 percentage points in January 1996. The actual contribution was twice as large. Thus, taking into account the reaction of other prices to changes in administered prices, this unexpected increase in administered prices explains about one-half of the 1996 price overshooting.

[16]There was also a problem of timing. The 1997 inflation target was announced in June 1996, when the 12–month inflation rate had just started declining. With the benefit of hindsight, that is, taking into account the drop in inflation in the second half of 1996, the announcement appears to have been premature.

in line with the revised target, the authorities' credibility was enhanced and this strengthened the prospects for a faster disinflation in 1998 and in the medium term (Chapter XIII).

References

Boote, Anthony R., and Janos Somogyi, 1991, *Economic Reform in Hungary Since 1968*, IMF Occasional Paper No. 83 (Washington: International Monetary Fund).

Kornai, János, 1997, "The Political Economy of the Hungarian Stabilization and Austerity Program," in *Macroeconomic Stabilization in Transition Economies*, by Mario I. Blejer and Marko Škreb (Cambridge, Massachusetts: Cambridge University Press), pp. 172–203.

Krueger, Thomas, and Mark S. Lutz, 1995, "Developments and Challenges in Hungary" in *Road Maps of the Transition—The Baltics, The Czech Republic, Hungary, and Russia*, by Biswajit Banerjee and others, IMF Occasional Paper No. 127 (Washington: International Monetary Fund).

National Bank of Hungary, 1994, "Consolidation of the Hungarian Banking System," Monthly Report (October).

Neményi, Judith, 1996, "Capital Inflow, Macroeconomic Equilibrium, the Public Debt and the Profit and Loss of the National Bank of Hungary," *Acta Oeconomica*, Vol. 48 (3–4), pp. 241–70.

III The External Current Account and Net Foreign Assets: Longer-Run Equilibrium Perspectives

Thomas Krueger and Carlo Cottarelli

The external current account in Hungary has been volatile during the transition period since 1989: small surpluses in the early years were followed by current account deficits of about 10 percent of GDP in 1993–94, and a subsequent strengthening with deficits averaging 3¼ percent of GDP during 1996–97 (Table 2.3 in Chapter II). From a saving-investment perspective, the relatively strong current account position in the earlier years reflected robust household saving but also weak investment demand in the wake of initial uncertainties surrounding the transition process (Table 2.2 in Chapter II). But with a considerable weakening in public and private sector savings, domestic saving was inadequate to finance the subsequent rebound in investment, leading to a substantial reliance on foreign saving. More recently, following the introduction of a policy adjustment package in early 1995, the current account deficit has dropped sharply: the 1997 deficit-to-GDP ratio is projected to be less than one-third of its 1994 level (Figure 3.1).

Developments in the current account have been mirrored to some extent by movements in real exchange rates, in particular, those based on unit labor cost (Figure 2.2 in Chapter II). The appreciation of the forint contributed, with some lag, to the deterioration of the current account in 1993/94 (although several other factors, including the impact of new bankruptcy regulations, were also important).[1] With product-based gross real wages declining by about 6½ percent during 1995–96, and concurrent substantial productivity gains, the gains in competitiveness were quickly reflected in a turnaround of the current account. These gains in competitiveness were also evidenced in strong gains in export market share that continued into 1997.

In parallel with the swings in the external current account, Hungary also witnessed relatively large movements in its foreign asset and debt position over the past seven years (Figure 3.1). The strong current account position at the beginning of the decade, as well as foreign direct investment inflows, contributed to a decline in the external debt-to-GDP ratio, which, however, by the end of 1992 remained well above levels in many other emerging markets—a legacy of the past. During 1993–94, sizable new net borrowing was needed to finance the current account deficit, and it was only in 1995 that the net debt ratio began to decline again, helped by the narrowing of the current account deficit and exceptionally large inflows of foreign direct investment, including privatization receipts. Even with its large external debt and debt service burden, Hungary has maintained its impeccable debt service record and, following policy adjustments since 1995, yield spreads have declined rapidly.

The volatility of the external account balance during the 1990s raises the issue of what level of this variable is broadly appropriate as a longer-term equilibrium. To address this issue, this chapter draws mainly on theoretical models that analyze the current account from an intertemporal saving-investment perspective. These models, which build on earlier work in the context of closed economies (for example, Lucas, 1981), highlight the role of the current account as a buffer against temporary shocks (such as a relative cyclical weakening or temporary negative supply shocks). But they also underscore the role of the current account in allocating resources in a more sustained way over time, for example, as a way of building up a country's foreign assets ahead of a relative aging of its population.

While the main focus of this approach is on flow equilibria, as reflected in the external current account, the approach also has implications for the cumulated sum of a country's historical current ac-

---

[1]As discussed in Chapters II and VI, these regulations forced many firms, including those in the export sector, to close down.

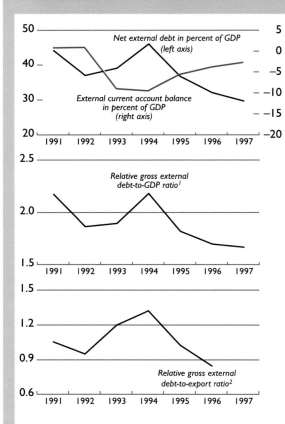

Figure 3.1. External Current Account Deficit and External Debt

Sources: International Monetary Fund, *World Economic Outlook*, 1997; and IMF staff calculations and projections.
[1]The figure reports the ratio between gross external debt (minus international reserves) and GDP in Hungary over the simple average of the same ratio computed for the countries classified in the *World Economic Outlook* as "market borrowers" or "countries without recent debt service difficulties." The figure for 1997 assumes that the ratio for the other countries is unchanged with respect to 1996.
[2]The figure reports the ratio between gross external debt (minus international reserves) and exports of goods and services in Hungary over the simple average of the same ratio computed for the countries classified in the *World Economic Outlook* as "market borrowers" or "countries without recent debt service difficulties."

change rate paths, and, in particular, on a recent study by Debelle and Faruqee (1996). Based on these results, simulations are presented that may provide a reference point for a current account or net foreign asset position.

Determinants of the External Current Account and Net Foreign Assets: Theoretical Aspects

Intertemporal Models of the Current Account as Saving-Investment Balance

External capital flows enable a country to import for some time more goods and services than it exports. Intertemporal solvency implies that these debts should eventually be repaid through surpluses on the trade and services accounts. In this way, the external current account is fundamentally a venue of intertemporal resource allocation between countries. This aspect is at the center of the approach that analyzes the current account within an intertemporal saving-investment model, and identifies the factors that may make it optimal for countries to run current account imbalances for some periods.

In addressing these issues, it is helpful to recall that net exports ($X–M$) have to equal ex post private sector saving (S^p) minus the sum of the government deficit (DEF) and private investment (I):[2]

$$S^p - DEF - I = X - M. \qquad (1)$$

Net exports is the national accounts equivalent to the external current account (CA), excluding transfers; for simplicity, it is assumed in this section that these transfers are zero so that the current account is equal to net exports.

The main focus of the intertemporal saving-investment approach is to identify the determinants of the left-hand side of equation (1), taking into account the intertemporal solvency condition of a country:

$$PV(CA) = - NFA_0, \qquad (2)$$

whereby the present value of all future current account balances, $PV(CA)$, must equal (the negative value of) a country's initial net foreign asset position. This allows a country with an initially positive net foreign asset position to "eat up" the assets over

counts, as reflected in the stock of external debt and foreign assets. Accordingly, in addition to analyzing the current account position, this chapter will also attempt to examine if, from cross-country comparisons, lessons can be drawn about Hungary's current net foreign asset position and its projected future path.

The chapter draws on ongoing analysis in the IMF on longer-run equilibrium current account and ex-

---

[2]Recall the national accounts identity that relates national income (Y) to the different demand components: $Y = C + I + G + X - M$. Equation (1) is derived directly from this identity, defining the government deficit (DEF)—on a national accounts basis—as $DEF = G - T$ and private sector saving as $S^p = (Y - C - T)$, where T denotes taxes net of transfers. $X - M$ includes (excludes) net factor payments if Y is based on gross national (gross domestic) income.

time by running current account deficits, and vice versa.

The intertemporal model highlights the role of the current account as buffer for *transitory shocks*. This essentially extends the consumption smoothing model to an open economy: among other things, it suggests a relatively strong current account position for a country that is in a weaker cyclical position than its trading partners; also, in the case of temporary real exchange rate, terms of trade, or supply shocks, demand smoothing would result in temporary current account imbalances. For example, an unusually bad harvest, as Hungary witnessed for several years in the early 1990s, may have only a limited effect on domestic demand and result in a concurrent temporary deterioration of the external current account.[3] Temporary shocks that affect the current account can also be policy induced, including monetary policy shocks and temporary changes in the fiscal policy stance.

The intertemporal approach also identifies factors that may result in more sustained periods of current account imbalances. A potentially important factor in this regard is a country's *relative stage of development*: a country that starts from a less-developed position, and is expected to narrow its relative income gap, could be expected to run a current account deficit during part of the catch-up period. While this would allow some intertemporal smoothing of consumption, it should also be reflected in a relatively large share of capital goods imports. As a result, the composition of a current account imbalance may be an important indicator of its sustainability. To some extent, these factors have an analogue on the capital account side. In particular, FDI-based financing may be able to sustain larger current account deficits or deficits for longer time periods.

Demographic factors may also result in sustained periods of current account imbalances. Theories in this respect mostly build on aggregate life-cycle models. In particular, as a country's population ages relative to its partner countries, its dependency ratio tends to rise; and if, as the life cycle hypothesis suggests, older dependent people have lower propensities to save, this would tend to lower a country's saving rate over time.[4] In order for the intertemporal solvency condition (2) to hold, this country would have to save relatively

more in the years prior to the relative rise in its dependency ratio, that is, ceteris paribus, a country would have to record a stronger current account position in the earlier years ahead of the relative aging of its population. Also, demographic developments can affect the fiscal position, for example, through their effect on the pension system. Let us, therefore, turn to the impact of fiscal policy on the current account.

Fiscal policy can affect the current account in these models through several channels (Frenkel and Razin, 1996). The fiscal deficit may affect a country's current account if Ricardian equivalence does not (fully) hold, so that changes in public sector saving are not fully offset by changes in private sector saving (see equation (1)). Fiscal policy also exerts direct demand effects (or indirect effects via taxation and transfers), and these have repercussions on the external current account. For example, to the extent that the private sector has a different (generally lower) marginal propensity to consume nontradable goods than the public sector, a temporary increase in government demand would affect the current account even if Ricardian equivalence held (Ostry, 1988).

The *real exchange rate* may also affect saving and investment directly and thereby the left-hand side of equation (1). While empirical evidence in this regard is at best mixed, the real exchange rate has generally a strong impact on external trade flows—that is, the right-hand side of equation (1)—as is captured in standard estimates of relative price elasticities for imports and exports. Therefore, in the empirical model employed in the next section, the real exchange rate is the key endogenous variable that ensures over the medium term ex ante balance between saving minus investment and the external current account, as captured by the two sides of equation (1).[5]

Finally, intertemporal models of the current account ascribe an important role to *interest rates* and, more generally, rates of return on assets. First, a rise in real interest rates has a wealth effect. It is negative in countries that are net borrowers, like Hungary, as it increases their debt service burden; as a result, Hungary would have to run larger current account (net of interest payments) surpluses over time if there were a sustained rise in real interest rates. Second, as an intertemporal price, the real interest rate also affects the intertemporal demand and supply pattern, and thereby the current account.

---

[3]However, to the extent that temporary shocks affect a country's net foreign asset position—for example, a temporary deterioration in the current account raises the external debt level and increases the future financing need—temporary shocks may also have longer-run implications for saving and investment and thereby the current account.

[4]Cross-section and cross-country evidence on the importance of these factors is mixed; see, for example, Poterba (1994), but also Masson, Bayoumi, and Samiei (1995).

[5]This role of the real exchange rate is a cornerstone of the macroeconomic balance approach, which goes back at least to Laursen and Metzler (1950), Harberger (1950), and Meade (1951). More recent analyses of the effect of real exchange rates on saving include Svensson and Razin (1983).

Foreign Asset Equilibria

The cumulated sum of a country's historical current accounts, adjusted for transfer payments and valuation gains, determines its net foreign asset position at any particular point in time. An alternative way to apply the intertemporal saving-investment model is, therefore, to focus on a country's net foreign asset position (i.e., a stock equilibrium) rather than the current account (i.e., a flow equilibrium). This may provide some additional insights, in particular in empirical work. For example, by analyzing the net foreign asset position, one can draw on the empirical observation that some, notably developing, countries have encountered (negative) net foreign asset positions that turned out to be ultimately unsustainable. The outstanding stock of net foreign assets may also provide an important indicator of a country's access to financial markets, an aspect that may not be adequately captured by an exclusive focus on current account flow developments.

With net foreign assets essentially representing the stock equivalent to the current account, the theoretical determinants of a country's optimal foreign asset position are closely related to the factors identified above in the intertemporal saving-investment model. In turn, net foreign assets have two important effects on a country's current account. First, the return on these assets directly affects the current account in the form of net interest and dividend payments as well as profit remittances. Second, net foreign asset positions should, over longer time periods, be reversed as indicated by the solvency condition (2) above. It has proven difficult to disentangle these two effects in empirical work on the saving-investment model. As a result, analyzing a country's foreign asset equilibrium directly may provide useful additional insights into a country's external position.

Model-Based Results and Cross-Country Comparisons

The theoretical framework of the previous section can now be applied to analyze the external equilibrium for Hungary. However, in view of the fairly short experience with a relatively liberalized balance of payments, the analysis to identify the longer-run importance of different variables has to rely largely on historical evidence and parameter estimates for other countries. These parameter estimates are applied in this section to Hungary and provide a benchmark against which one can assess Hungary's developments and prospects.

The analysis in this section draws extensively on a recent study by Debelle and Faruqee (1996). Covering 1971–93, they provide an empirical investigation of the external current account and net foreign asset determinants for a large set of countries, including 21 industrial countries and 34 other, mainly developing, countries. Their panel data study, which does not include Hungary, uses cross-section analysis—where each country is treated as a single observation—as well as time series panel data—where also the behavior over time in the different countries is analyzed.

Intertemporal Saving-Investment Model

Based on the econometric relations estimated by Debelle and Faruqee (1996), the following equation can be used to derive a benchmark value for the medium-term equilibrium value of the external current account in Hungary:[6]

$$CA = -1.91 - 0.13DEF - 0.04DEP + \alpha DEVREL. \tag{3}$$

Here, the current account depends on three factors: the general government deficit-to-GDP ratio (DEF), the dependency ratio (DEP), and a country's relative stage of development ($DEVREL$). The parameter estimates in equation (3) suggest that a decline in the general government deficit-to-GDP ratio by 1 percentage point would tend to raise the current account balance by 0.13 percentage point of GDP, an estimate that indicates a small deviation from Ricardian equivalence.[7] One issue that needs to be solved in deriving estimates for the equilibrium current account is which value of the fiscal deficit should be used in equation (3). The solution used here is to use the maximum deficit that would be consistent with a "sustainable" path of the public-debt-to-GDP ratio, that is, with keeping the debt ratio constant at a level of about 60 percent of GDP (not far from the average level at which the Hungarian authorities intend to keep the public debt ratio in the next five years; see Ministry of Finance and others, 1997). This approach has the advantage of focusing on values of the fiscal and external deficits that are consistent with both the intertemporal budget constraint of the country and with the intertemporal budget constraint of the government.[8]

---

[6]Debelle and Faruqee (1996) report several estimates for industrial as well as for developing countries. Equation (3) is based on one of their estimates for developing countries (see column (3) of Table A2 in their paper); using other specifications yields in most cases quite similar results for Hungary's benchmark current account level; also see Krueger (1996).

[7]Other specifications in Debelle and Faruqee (1996) yield sometimes larger deviations from Ricardian equivalence. Also, note that, in contrast to the fiscal deficit, government expenditures were not found to be a statistically significant determinant of the current account.

[8]This yields a fiscal deficit of about 4 percent of GDP, after adjusting for inflation. Note that the operational deficit implicit in the Hungarian authorities' medium-term scenario is lower, as the authorities target a decline in the public debt ratio. Thus, using

The relative dependency ratio of a country is also estimated to have a significant effect on the current account. As predicted by the model discussed in the previous section, countries with a relatively small dependency ratio tend to have stronger current account positions, with a 1 percentage point rise in the dependency ratio estimated to result in a 0.04 percentage point decline in the current account-to-GDP ratio. At present, Hungary's dependency ratio is below the developing country average underlying the parameter estimates in equation (3)—reflecting the large proportion of underaged youth in developing countries—with some relative increase expected over the next five years.[9]

The empirical model of equation (3) also indicates that the relative stage of development has an important effect on the current account. In the estimates of Debelle and Faruqee (1996), this variable is proxied by a country's relative income and relative capital stock position.[10] This effect tends to strengthen the estimated current account balance in the case of Hungary, especially in view of its larger estimated capital stock compared with many developing countries.

Using the parameters in equation (3) yields a benchmark current account deficit for 1996 of 3¾ percent of GDP. This value is close to the actual deficit registered that year and somewhat larger than the one expected in 1997 (Figure 3.1). Thus, the authorities' adjustment policies after March 1995 succeeded in lowering the external deficit to a level that can be regarded as broadly consistent with the structural features of the Hungarian economy, based on cross-country comparisons.

The above results should, of course, be taken with caution, for two reasons. First, the state of the art of empirical work in this area does not generate econo-

metric estimates that can be put into narrow confidence bands. Indeed, some other parameter estimates presented by Debelle and Faruqee (1996) would yield a somewhat lower benchmark current account deficit for Hungary (Krueger, 1996). Second, the model estimated by Debelle and Faruqee (1996) does not take into account some factors that may be important for Hungary, as well as for other transition economies. For example, the capital requirement of transition economies may be temporarily higher than in other economies, because of the need to rebuild the capital stock (Krueger, 1996). Another aspect concerns the composition of the financing of the current account deficit. As noted above, foreign direct investment may allow for sustaining larger external imbalances for longer periods of time, as they typically tend to be less volatile than other forms of external financing.[11] Of course, this conclusion should not be drawn to the extreme of ignoring altogether the long-run implications of FDI, for example, for the service component of the external current account.[12]

The above-described econometric estimates also provide some indications of how the external current account should move in time, as the determinants of the current account in equation (3) are not fixed. Based on projections for these determinants,[13] the benchmark external current account would be expected to decline over time (on average by about ¼ of a percentage point of GDP a year in the six years starting in 1996; as noted, the improvement expected in 1997 is larger than this amount). Such a decline reflects the relatively rapid increase in per capita income and the capital stock projected by the authorities (per capita income is expected to rise by almost 4 percent a year during 1997–2002). This would be only partially offset by a projected concurrent deterioration in the dependency ratio relative to developing countries.

Stock of Net Foreign Asset

Hungary's net external debt position has improved rapidly since 1994. Net external debt is projected to be slightly above 29 percent of GDP at the end of

---

the actual fiscal targets would yield lower values for the benchmark current account deficit. Finally, note that the inclusion in equation (3) of the fiscal deficit by no means implies that any increase in the fiscal deficit would raise the level of the sustainable normal external deficit. A fiscal deficit level that was inconsistent with the government's intertemporal budget constraint could lead to an unsustainable deterioration of the external accounts.

[9]The dependency ratio is defined here as the sum of the number of people under 19 and above 65, divided by the rest of the population. This understates the ratio in cases where the mandatory retirement age is below 65 or a portion of the working age population is not employed. Particularly in comparison with some industrial countries, these factors may be relatively important in Hungary, although the recently introduced pension reform could be expected to alleviate some of these effects; see also the discussion in Chapter V. It should also be noted that the dependency ratio is only a rough approximation of the intertemporal demographic factors suggested by theoretical economic models, as discussed earlier.

[10]Their specification included level and square terms for both variables. When only the relative income level is included in the regression, the coefficient α is positive, as expected in the theoretical model of the previous section.

---

[11]For example, results reported in Frankel and Rose (1996) suggest that the share of FDI in total debt tends to lower the probability of a currency crash in emerging markets.

[12]FDI, like any other external liability, entails profit remittances. However, in most countries, reinvested profits from FDI are not fully captured in the external current account. This lowers the measured current account deficit in countries, like Hungary, that have net FDI liabilities (and it correspondingly underestimates FDI). Note that, as in other countries, the Hungarian official statistics include the cumulated sum of FDI in the country's external liabilities.

[13]All projections and targets for Hungary are based on Ministry of Finance and others (1997).

1997, against 45 percent of GDP at the end of 1994.[14] Moreover, reflecting the intense activity of foreign exchange intervention since March 1995 (Chapter II), net public external debt has declined even more rapidly.

There has been a strong improvement also relative to other countries during this period. Cross-country comparisons of external debt are fraught with statistical difficulties, as in many countries the information on external assets and liabilities of the private sector is incomplete. With this caveat, and based on available data in the World Economic Outlook database, Figure 3.1 shows the gross debt (net of official reserves)-to-GDP ratio in Hungary relative to a large group of emerging economies. In the early 1990s and through 1994, the external debt ratio in Hungary was about twice as large as in the emerging market group. This reflected not only the large external imbalances that had characterized the 1980s but also the fact that Hungary had continued to service its debt impeccably, while other countries in the group had undertaken debt renegotiations. Hungary's external debt-to-GDP ratio dropped much faster than in the emerging market group during 1995–97, although at the end of 1997, it is projected to remain well above the average. This fact is, however, mitigated by several factors, including Hungary's fairly small share of short-term debt (about 12 percent of total debt at the end of 1996). Furthermore, Hungary's external position ranks better based on other relative debt indicators. In particular, reflecting the relative openness of its economy, Hungary's ratio of external debt to exports had fallen well below the ratio for the emerging market group at the end of 1996 (and probably further below the average in 1997).[15]

What are the implications for the external debt-to-GDP ratio of the improvement in the external current account observed through 1997? In spite of the expected fall in privatization receipts from abroad after 1997, it is reasonable to assume that in the medium term, FDI could continue to offset external current account deficit of the order of magnitude of the one observed for 1997. In this case, external debt would stabilize in dollar terms and would fall in relation to GDP. Assuming an average growth rate of 5½ percent (see Chapter VI), the external debt-to-GDP ratio would drop to 22½ percent by 2002.

A further decline in the external debt ratio is consistent with the expected trends in Hungary's fundamentals, based on parameter estimates in Debelle and Faruqee (1996). Their estimates suggest the following long-run determinants of a country's net external debt position:

$$Net\ debt = CONST + 0.57GDEBT + 0.45DEP \\ - 0.53YREP, \qquad (4)$$

where net debt is determined by the ratio of government debt-to-GDP (*GDEBT*) as well as a country's dependency ratio (*DEP*) and relative per capita income (*YREP*). For example, a decline in the government debt ratio of 10 percentage points is estimated to be associated with a reduction in net debt of 5.7 percent of GDP; this relationship between the stock of foreign debt and government debt corresponds to the earlier discussed relationship between the current account and government deficits.[16]

These estimates would imply that a further decline in Hungary's external debt should be expected, as a result of changes in all three right-hand-side variables in equation (4): a sustained decline of the public-debt-to-GDP ratio, reflecting a gradual reduction in the budget deficit and robust GDP growth targeted by the authorities; the targeted narrowing in the income gap; and a (temporary) decline in Hungary's dependency ratio relative to industrial countries.

References

Artus, Jacques R., 1978, "Methods of Assessing the Long-Run Equilibrium Value of an Exchange Rate," *Journal of International Economics*, Vol. 8, pp. 277–99.

Debelle, Guy, and Hamid Faruqee, 1996, "What Determines the Current Account? A Cross-Sectional and Panel Approach," IMF Working Paper No. 96/58 (Washington: International Monetary Fund).

Edwards, Sebastian, 1989, *Real Exchange Rates, Devaluation, and Adjustment: Exchange Rate Policy in Developing Countries* (Cambridge, Massachusetts: MIT Press).

Frankel, Jeffrey A., and Andrew K. Rose, 1996, "Currency Crashes in Emerging Markets: An Empirical Treatment," *Journal of International Economics*, Vol. 41, pp. 351–66.

---

[14]Net external debt would be about 3½ percentage points of GDP lower, excluding intercompany loans.

[15]Recent empirical research (Manzocchi, 1997) suggests that the export-to-GDP ratio is a key factor in determining a country's access to international capital markets. Another traditional indicator of a country's external position is the debt service ratio. However, in countries with an active debt management policy, such as Hungary, this indicator has to be interpreted with caution, as it is highly sensitive to changes in the schedule of debt amortization related, inter alia, to early repayments. In particular, the debt service ratio for Hungary has remained high in 1995 and 1996 because of early repayments or refinancing of outstanding loans.

---

[16]Note that equation (4) is estimated by Debelle and Faruqee (1996) for all net external liabilities, including those arising from FDI. At the end of 1996, the stock of foreign direct investment in Hungary was estimated at about 30 percent of GDP. However, as discussed above, there are good reasons for a separate treatment of FDI stocks.

Frenkel, Jacob A., and Assaf Razin, 1996, *Fiscal Policies and the World Economy* (Cambridge, Massachusetts: MIT Press, 3rd ed.).

Harberger, Arnold C., 1950, "Currency Depreciation, Income and the Balance of Trade," *Journal of Political Economy*, Vol. 58 (February), pp. 47–60.

International Monetary Fund, 1997, *World Economic Outlook* (Washington: International Monetary Fund).

Isard, Peter, 1995, *Exchange Rate Economics* (Cambridge, England; New York, N.Y.: Cambridge University Press).

Krueger, Thomas, 1996, "The External Current Account and Net Foreign Assets in Hungary: Longer-Run Equilibrium Perspectives," in *Hungary—Selected Issues*, IMF Staff Country Report No. 96/109 (Washington: International Monetary Fund).

Laursen, Svend, and Lloyd A. Metzler, 1950, "Flexible Exchange Rates and the Theory of Employment," *Review of Economics and Statistics*, Vol. 32, pp. 281–99.

Lipschitz, Leslie, and Donogh McDonald, 1992, "Real Exchange Rates and Competitiveness: A Clarification of Concepts and Some Measurement for Europe," *Empirica*, Vol. 19, pp. 37–69.

Lucas, Robert E. Jr., 1981, *Studies in Business-Cycle Theory* (Cambridge, Massachusetts: MIT Press).

Manzocchi, Stefano, 1997, "External Finance and Foreign Debt in Central and Eastern European Countries," IMF Working Paper No. 97/134 (Washington: International Monetary Fund).

Masson, Paul R., Tamim Bayoumi, and Hossein Samiei, 1995, "International Evidence on the Determinants of Private Saving," IMF Working Paper No. 95/51 (Washington: International Monetary Fund).

Meade, James E., 1951, *The Theory of International Economic Policy: The Balance of Payments*, Vol. 1 (London; New York: Oxford University Press).

Ministry of Finance and Directorate-General for Economic and Financial Affairs of the European Commission, June 1997, *Joint Assessment of Hungary's Medium-Term Economic Policy Priorities* (Budapest).

Ostry, Jonathan D., 1988, "The Balance of Trade, Terms of Trade, and Real Exchange Rate," *Staff Papers*, International Monetary Fund, Vol. 35 (December), pp. 541–73.

Poterba, James M. (ed.), 1994, *International Comparisons of Household Saving*, NBER Report Series (Chicago: University of Chicago).

Rogoff, Kenneth, 1996, "The Purchasing Power Parity Puzzle," *Journal of Economic Literature*, Vol. 34, No. 2 (June), pp. 647–68.

Svensson, Lars E. O., and Assaf Razin, 1983, "The Terms of Trade and the Current Account: The Harberger-Laursen-Metzler Effect," *Journal of Political Economy*, Vol. 91 (February), pp. 91–125.

Williamson, John, 1985, *The Exchange Rate System* (Washington: Institute for International Economics, 2nd ed.).

IV Public Debt Dynamics and Fiscal Solvency

Reza Moghadam

Hungary's public debt-to-GDP ratio, a key indicator of the state of public finances, has fluctuated widely during the 1990s. The gross debt of the consolidated central government[1] rose from about 66 percent of GDP in 1990 to nearly 90 percent of GDP in 1993, before declining gradually to below 85 percent of GDP in 1995.[2] There has been a sharp decline in the debt-to-GDP ratio since 1995 (Figure 4.1, top panel). By the end of the century, the authorities intend to reduce this ratio to well below the 60 percent level specified in the Maastricht Treaty, as a condition for participating in the European Monetary Union.

One factor behind the rise in the debt ratio in the early 1990s was undoubtedly the deteriorating fiscal position of the government (Chapter II). However, when analyzing government debt dynamics in Hungary, a number of special factors have to be taken into account in addition to the government's fiscal position. For example, during 1992–94, the government issued substantial amounts of bonds to recapitalize state banks and to cover losses from earlier housing loans, adding to the debt burden. Since 1994, the government has benefited from considerable privatization revenue, which has mainly been used to reduce government debt. Another important factor affecting debt dynamics in Hungary is the interest rate charged on debt. A small component of domestic debt, related to central bank credit to government prior to 1991, carries a below-market interest rate. More importantly, until this year, a large part of the debt stock consisted of zero-interest-bearing liabilities to the National Bank of Hungary arising from the devaluation losses associated with the foreign debt, contracted in the past by the central

bank on behalf of the government (Figure 4.1, bottom panel). This portion of the debt did not bear any interest. On January 1, 1997, through a so-called securitization operation, the government swapped the stock of the non-interest-bearing valuation losses

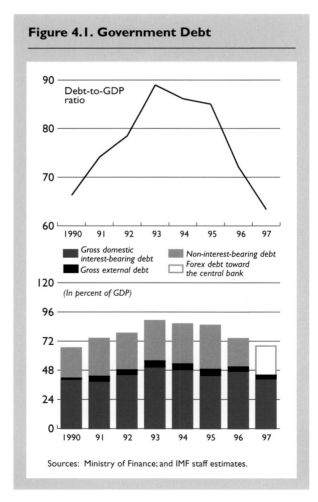

Figure 4.1. Government Debt

Debt-to-GDP ratio

■ Gross domestic interest-bearing debt
■ Gross external debt
▨ Non-interest-bearing debt
□ Forex debt toward the central bank

(In percent of GDP)

Sources: Ministry of Finance; and IMF staff estimates.

---

[1]Including the non-interest-bearing liabilities vis-à-vis the National Bank of Hungary for valuation losses (see below). These liabilities were roughly of the same magnitude as the net foreign debt position of the central bank.

[2]Consolidated central government excludes the local governments (see Chapter V for further details). References to government in this section refer only to the consolidated government.

Table 4.1. Decomposition of the Change in Debt[1]
(Contribution to change in debt, in percent)

	1992	1993	1994	1995	1996	Estimate 1997	1992–97
Change in debt (I+II)	100.0	100.0	100.0	100.0	100.0	100.0	100.0
I. Consolidated deficit (1–2–3)	46.8	32.9	51.5	36.4	106.8	73.6	48.7
1. Total interest payments	35.8	18.8	47.9	50.9	284.8	140.8	67.0
2. Primary surplus excluding interest revenue	−13.4	−14.4	−4.6	12.2	163.4	47.7	13.5
3. Interest revenue	2.3	0.4	1.0	2.3	14.5	19.5	4.8
II. Other items (1+...+6)	53.2	67.1	48.5	63.6	−6.8	26.4	51.3
1. Consolidation bonds and other debt-generating operations	28.5	34.3	10.7	5.9	12.8	0.0	15.7
Consolidation bonds	28.5	34.3	8.4	0.6	4.5	0.0	13.4
Other	0.0	0.0	2.3	5.3	0.0	0.0	2.3
2. Impact of devaluation	27.7	43.0	58.1	75.2	69.3	52.5	55.2
3. Privatization receipts	−2.6	−2.6	−10.0	−15.6	−107.8	−9.5	−14.2
4. Change in the treasury account	...	3.2	−10.5	−0.9	27.9	−15.9	−2.0
5. Other asset reducing operations[2]	0.0	−8.9	0.0	0.0	0.0	0.0	−2.1
6. Other	−0.4	−1.8	0.2	−1.0	−9.0	−0.7	−1.3

Sources: Data provided by the Hungarian authorities; and IMF staff calculations.

[1]The calculations in this table are based on data provided to IMF staff in June 1997.

[2]Import of military equipment using claims against Russia. The 1993 deficit is inflated by the same amount with respect to the cash deficit figure.

with foreign exchange denominated liabilities to the central bank.[3] In fact, the operation was designed to ensure that the new stock of National Bank of Hungary foreign exchange claims on the government was identical, in size and maturity, to the net foreign exchange position of the central bank. This chapter analyzes the above factors and quantifies their contribution to determining debt dynamics in Hungary. It then proceeds to draw conclusions regarding the conditions that need to be met to prevent an increase in the debt-to-GDP ratio. This is important because a debt ratio that is not increasing is a condition for the solvency of public finances, that is, for the government to meet its intertemporal budget constraint.

Determinants of Debt Dynamics

The change in debt can be expressed in the following form:

$$\Delta D = (I{-}P) + A \qquad (1)$$

where I is interest payments; P is the primary surplus; and A is other items besides the budget deficit

that affect indebtedness, for example, privatization receipts, devaluation losses, and issuance of bonds for recapitalizing banks.

Table 4.1 provides the breakdown of the change in debt since 1992 according to equation (1). It also identifies the major components of A. The table confirms that the fiscal deficit has had a significant impact on debt, accounting for about one-half of the increase in debt during 1992–97 (see last column of Table 4.1). Other items have also played an important role in explaining the movements in debt. For example, the issuance of consolidation bonds in 1992 and 1993 accounts for about one-third of the increase in debt during that period. Another critical element in explaining the increase in debt is the devaluation of the exchange rate: the contribution of this element has been of the same order of magnitude as the deficit.

Privatization receipts have had a significant role in limiting the increase in debt. For 1992–97 as a whole, the rise in debt would have been about 14 percent higher in the absence of privatization. Finally, in some years, the change in government deposits has also been an important component of A. In 1994, for instance, government deposits were drawn down substantially, while in 1996, there was a significant buildup of these deposits.

Equation (1) is useful in helping to identify the key determinants of the change in nominal debt; however,

[3]See International Monetary Fund (1996), Chapter IV. The term "securitization" is the literal translation of the Hungarian expression to describe this operation. It is somewhat misleading as there was no actual transfer of securities between the central bank and the government.

Table 4.2. Decomposition of the Change in Debt-to-GDP Ratio[1]
(Percentage points, unless otherwise indicated)

	1992	1993	1994	1995	1996	1997	1994–97
Change in d (I+II+III)	4.3	10.4	−2.8	−0.8	−11.0	−6.0	−20.7
I.1 Primary deficit, p (excluding interest revenue)[2]	2.1	3.4	0.6	−2.2	−4.9	−3.1	−9.5
I.2 Interest revenue[3]	−0.4	−0.1	−0.1	−0.4	−0.4	−1.3	−2.3
II. $(i − g)/(1 + g)*d_{-1}$	−1.4	1.3	−1.9	3.8	−3.5	0.1	−1.5
III. Other items (a)	3.9	5.7	−1.3	−2.0	−2.3	−1.7	−7.4
Consolidation bonds and other debt- generating operations	4.4	8.1	1.5	1.0	0.4	0.0	2.9
Privatization revenue	−0.4	−0.6	−1.4	−2.8	−3.2	−0.6	−8.0
Changes in treasury account deposits	. . .	0.8	−1.5	−0.2	0.8	−1.0	−1.8
Asset-reducing operations[4]	0.0	−2.1	0.0	0.0	0.0	0.0	0.0
Other	−0.1	−0.4	0.0	−0.2	−0.3	0.0	−0.5
Memorandum items:							
Effective interest rate, i (percent)	15.6	22.6	20.3	33.0	14.9	20.6	. . .
Growth rate of nominal GDP, g (percent)	17.8	20.6	23.0	27.4	19.7	20.5	. . .

Sources: Data provided by the Hungarian authorities; and IMF staff calculations.

[1]This table is based on data provided to IMF staff in June 1997; more recent information reported in Figure 4.1 indicates that the fall in the debt-to-GDP ratio in 1997 was larger than reported in this table, owing to stronger GDP growth and higher privatization receipts. Because of revisions in the GDP series, the changes in the debt ratio reported in this table for 1992–96 may also differ from those reported in Figure 4.1, in Table 4.3, and in Chapter II.

[2]A negative sign indicates a surplus. These figures differ from those reported in Box 2.1 of Chapter II because the primary balance here is defined as inclusive of the profit transfers from the National Bank of Hungary and of the transfers to the National Bank of Hungary to cover losses. Moreover, the figure in Chapter II refers to a broader definition of public sector and is adjusted for various factors (see Box 2.1 in Chapter II).

[3]Interest revenues mostly reflect the remuneration of the treasury account held by the government at the National Bank of Hungary.

[4]Import of military equipment using claims against Russia.

to facilitate an analysis of debt dynamics and the sustainability of debt, it is useful to rewrite equation (1) in terms of ratios to GDP. Dividing both sides of equation (1) by Y, the nominal GDP, and defining:

$$I = i\, D_{-1} ; \qquad (2a)$$

and

$$Y = (1+g)Y_{-1} \qquad (2b)$$

where i is the nominal interest rate and g is the growth rate of nominal GDP, we obtain:

$$D/Y − D_{-1}/[(1+g)Y_{-1}] = i\, D_{-1}/[(1+g)Y_{-1}] − P/Y + A/Y \qquad (3)$$

Equation (3) can be rewritten as:

$$\Delta d = −p + (i−g)d_{-1}/(1+g) + a \qquad (4)$$

where $d = D/Y$, $p = P/Y$, and $a = A/Y$.

Equation (4) decomposes the change in the debt-to-GDP ratio into the primary deficit ($−p$), a component reflecting the difference between interest rate and growth rate ($i−g$), and a component reflecting temporary factors (a).

Table 4.2 provides the decomposition of Δd, the change in the debt-to-GDP ratio, according to equation (4). The primary surplus was in fact negative during 1992–94, contributing to the rise in the debt ratio. The fiscal adjustment process since 1995 has meant that the magnitude of the primary surplus has been one of the key factors explaining the decline in the debt ratio over the past three years. In fact, the size of the primary balance explains about one-half of the 20 percentage point drop in the debt-to-GDP ratio since 1994 (see the last column of Table 4.2).

The other component of equation (4), which has had a significant impact on the decline in the debt ratio since 1994, has been a. This component had a positive impact in 1992 and 1993, mainly because of the issuance of capitalization bonds; however, since 1994, a has been negative, thanks mainly to privatization receipts.

To calculate the contribution of the second term in equation (4), that is, $(i−g)d_{-1}/(1+g)$, we have to calculate the effective interest rate on debt, i. To do this, we have added the devaluation losses to the actual domestic interest payments in equation (2a).[4] Nonetheless, $i−g$ turns out to be negative in a number of years, reflecting mainly the fact that the for-

---

[4]In contrast to Table 4.1, devaluation losses are not included as a separate item in the presentation in Table 4.2.

eign exchange liabilities vis-à-vis the National Bank of Hungary did not bear any interest.[5] Only in 1993 and 1995, when the forint depreciated sharply, does the contribution of $(i-g)d_{-1}/(1+g)$ become positive.[6] This term is also positive in 1997, albeit small in magnitude, reflecting the debt swap operation between the National Bank of Hungary and the government, which replaced the zero-interest-bearing debt with foreign exchange liabilities vis-à-vis the central bank. Since part of the forint debt vis-à-vis the National Bank of Hungary bears a below-market interest rate and the full impact of the securitization operation on interest payments will not be felt on the budget until 1998, and considering the low level of devaluation losses in 1997, the contribution of $(i-g)d_{-1}/(1+g)$ is small in 1997.

When looking at the solvency of the public sector and the long-term sustainability of the debt ratio in perspective, it is necessary to assume that $i-g$ will be positive.[7] Indeed, the proportion of below-market interest-bearing debt in Hungary is rapidly declining and market interest rates, at which treasury bills and government bonds are issued, are currently comfortably positive in real terms. Similarly, in the medium term, any contribution from a should not be expected.[8] Therefore, any analysis of future debt dynamics and sustainability would have to focus on the first two right-hand terms in equation (4), namely, p and $(i-g)d_{-1}/(1+g)$.

Debt Sustainability

Equation (4) implies that for the debt-to-GDP ratio to stabilize the primary surplus has to be larger than $(i-g)d_{-1}/(1+g)$, assuming no contribution from a. Although the debt-to-GDP ratio in Hungary declined in 1994, this was achieved by using privatization receipts and running down government deposits (Tables 4.1 and 4.2). The government was running a primary deficit and $i-g$ was negative—not a sustainable situation in the long run. In fact, in 1994, before the economic adjustment process began, Hungary was

---

[5]Also, as mentioned above, part of the forint debt vis-à-vis the National Bank of Hungary carries a below-market interest rate.

[6]Interest payments on consolidation bonds also increased sharply in 1995.

[7]If $i-g$ is negative, then the government debt can grow faster than the real resource base of the economy. More formally, if $i-g$ is negative, then the economy would be "dynamically inefficient," i.e., the return to capital in each period would be less than the amount of resources devoted to capital formation (see Buiter, 1997). The fact that $(i-g)$ was negative in Hungary for most of the 1990s reflects primarily the below-market interest rate paid by the government to the National Bank of Hungary.

[8]The government, however, has recently amended the privatization law to facilitate the sale of the remaining minority shareholding in a number of enterprises.

Table 4.3. Analysis of Debt Sustainability
(In percent, unless otherwise indicated)

	1994	1997
Debt stock (in billions of forint)	3,800	5,300
Domestic	2,100	3,200
Foreign	1,700	2,000
Debt/GDP	85	64
Marginal interest rate, i	28	22
Nominal GDP growth rate, g	23	20
$(i-g)$	5.0	2.0
Required primary surplus $(i-g)d_{-1}/(1+g)$	3.5	1.1
Actual primary surplus, p[1]	−0.6	3.1

Sources: Data provided by the Hungarian authorities; and IMF staff calculations.

[1]Excludes interest revenues. With interest revenues and excluding some misclassified items, the primary surplus would be −0.5 percent of GDP in 1994 and 4.1 percent of GDP in 1997.

probably in a debt trap. This is illustrated by column 1 in Table 4.3. Using the actual debt stock and nominal GDP growth, and an interest rate in domestic currency close to those prevailing in the market on new debt issues in 1994, column 1 indicates that the government would have needed to run a primary surplus of at least 3½ percent of GDP to stabilize the debt ratio in 1994. In fact, the 1994 budget entailed a primary deficit of about ½ percent of GDP.

A similar calculation for 1997 implies a required primary surplus of only just over 1 percent of GDP, against an actual primary surplus (excluding interest revenue) of about 3 percent of GDP.[9]

One other issue has to be taken into account in this analysis: seigniorage. In theory, seigniorage would reduce the primary balance needed for the debt-to-GDP ratio to decline. Estimates based on the forint-denominated component of reserve money, prevailing market interest rates, and interest rates on the required reserves put the magnitude of seigniorage at about 3½ percent of GDP in 1994 and at about 2½ percent of GDP in 1996.[10] Seigniorage is likely to decline further in 1997, and it is unlikely to exceed ½–1 percent of GDP in the medium term. If these estimates of seigniorage were included in Table 4.3, the basic results would remain unchanged.

---

[9]The primary surplus is somewhat lower in the more comprehensive definition used in Chapter II.

[10]The decline in seigniorage can be attributed to lower inflation, the drop in interest rates, and lower demand for base money.

According to the table, Hungary would have needed a primary surplus of 3½ percent of GDP in 1994 to stabilize its debt ratio; even if we subtract ½–1 percentage point as the medium-term value of seigniorage, the required primary surplus would have still been much higher than the actual primary deficit of ½ percent of GDP.[11] Therefore, the situation was not sustainable even taking into account seigniorage. In 1997, the actual primary surplus is higher than that required for debt stabilization; therefore, the magnitude of seigniorage is immaterial in terms of debt sustainability.

Conclusion

The analysis of the debt dynamics presented here indicates that:

(1) the debt-to-GDP ratio was not on a sustainable trajectory in 1994;

(2) the fiscal consolidation undertaken since 1995 has played a key role in reducing the debt ratio in Hungary; nonetheless, a sizable decline in the debt ratio over the last three years can be attributed to other items, in particular, privatization; and

(3) the primary surplus in 1997 is adequate to ensure a downward trend in the debt ratio. The authorities' medium-term strategy envisages a drop of about 1½ percent of GDP in the primary surplus in 1998 and maintaining the surplus in the following four years. Despite this decline, the magnitude of the primary surplus should be sufficient to keep the debt-to-GDP ratio on a downward trajectory, even ignoring seigniorage and the privatization revenues, which are likely to materialize in the next few years. Indeed, as the debt-to-GDP ratio drops, the primary surplus needed to ensure its continued decline becomes smaller than the value calculated here for 1997.

---

[11]Moreover, the primary balance reported in the table already includes part of seigniorage revenues (those consisting of transfers of central bank profits to the government). The component of seigniorage that was not included corresponds to those transfers that took the form of interest payments on the treasury account held by the government at the central bank (the bulk of the interest revenues in item I.2 of Table 4.2).

References

Buiter, Willem, H., 1997, "Aspects of Fiscal Performance in Some Transition Economies Under Fund-Supported Programs," IMF Working Paper No. 97/31 (Washington: International Monetary Fund).

International Monetary Fund, 1996, *Hungary—Selected Issues*, IMF Staff Country Report No. 96/109 (Washington: International Monetary Fund).

V Reform of Public Finances, 1994–97

Edgardo Ruggiero

During 1994–97, Hungary implemented far-reaching structural changes in the area of public finance, and has achieved both a considerable contraction in the size of the government and sizable primary surpluses. This chapter first describes the main institutional characteristics of the government sector and the principal issues that policymakers had to address; then it reviews the reforms and their effect on fiscal indicators.[1]

Size and Composition of Government and Main Structural Problems

In 1994, the state of public finances was characterized by both a large deficit and revenue and expenditure ratios that were high by international standards. As discussed in Chapter IV, the primary balance was negative (Figure 5.1), and in the presence of a sizable public debt, the underlying dynamics of the debt-to-GDP ratio was not sustainable. The size of the central government was also particularly large, in terms of both expenditure and revenue ratios to GDP. Total revenues (excluding privatization receipts) were 48¼ percent of GDP, while total expenditures were 55½ percent of GDP. Such expenditure ratios are large compared with the OECD average (38½ percent).[2] Government employment, as a percent of total employment in the economy, was also larger than in most OECD countries in the early 1990s (Figure 5.2). Also, Hungary had a relatively large civil service compared with other central and eastern European countries (Figure 5.3).

The bloated size of public finances and its large deficit reflected underlying weaknesses in several public sector areas, including a complex informa-tional and institutional structure and inefficient and unsustainable pension, health, and subsidy systems.

Informational and Institutional Structure

Fiscal policy management was hampered by inadequate information and complex institutional structures. The central government comprised (and still comprises) four groups of entities: the State Budget (SB), the Central Budgetary Institutions (CBIs) with budgetary autonomy, the Extrabudgetary Funds (EBFs), and the self-governing Social Security Funds (SSFs) (Box 5.1). These entities pursue their institutional objectives and are endowed with their own revenue-raising abilities, within the confines of their instituting laws and the yearly budget law. The CBIs have their own independent revenue sources that, until 1996, were not remitted to a central treasury account, though they were taken into account when measuring the budget deficit.[3] The SSFs were, for financial and policy purposes, controlled directly by Parliament, with the Ministry of Finance formally responsible only for commenting on their budgets when these were presented for approval to Parliament. Several transfers and payments took (and still take) place among these entities.[4] Partly because of the complexity of intergovernmental flows and the institutional independence of these entities, the compilation of consolidated revenues and expenditure in either an economic or a functional classification has been extremely difficult. This has been an obstacle in fully assessing the economic impact of government policies.

---

[1]The focus is on the consolidated central government as defined in Box 5.1. This definition is narrower than the definition of public sector used in Chapter II, which covered local governments, the state privatization agency (APV Rt), and the central bank.

[2]The average expenditure figure is based on the 22 OECD countries for which 1994 consolidated central government data from International Monetary Fund (1996) are available.

[3]Until 1995, the CBIs were allowed to purchase government securities and treat the interest revenue as their own resources.

[4]For example, the Central Budget makes transfers to the Extra-budgetary Funds for nationally relevant investments, pays social insurance contributions on the salaries of its employees to the SSFs and the EBFs, and transfers figurative amounts to the SSFs for coverage of the population exempt from social insurance contributions; the Labor Market Fund (an EBF) pays social security contributions to the Pension Fund (an SSF) for the unemployment benefits that it disburses; the Health Fund (the other SSF) transfers funds to the CBIs and to local governments for financing the hospitals that are owned by the latter. There are also internal transfers and payments among EBFs, SSFs, and CBIs.

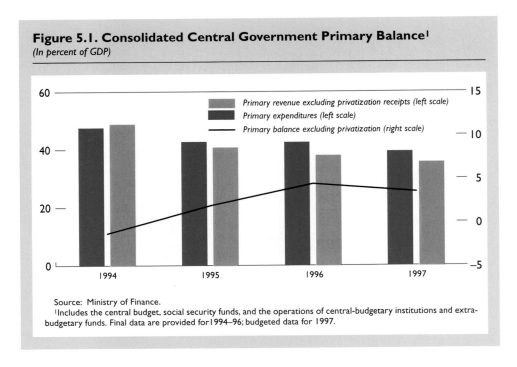

Figure 5.1. Consolidated Central Government Primary Balance[1]
(In percent of GDP)

Source: Ministry of Finance.
[1]Includes the central budget, social security funds, and the operations of central-budgetary institutions and extra-budgetary funds. Final data are provided for 1994–96; budgeted data for 1997.

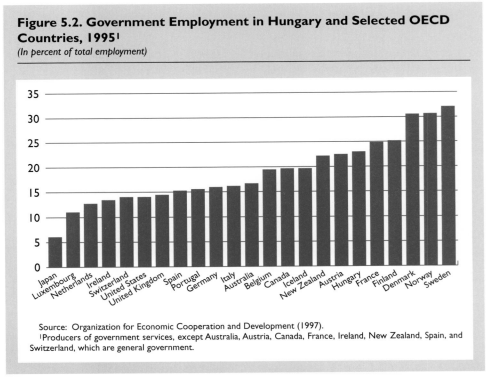

Figure 5.2. Government Employment in Hungary and Selected OECD Countries, 1995[1]
(In percent of total employment)

Source: Organization for Economic Cooperation and Development (1997).
[1]Producers of government services, except Australia, Austria, Canada, France, Ireland, New Zealand, Spain, and Switzerland, which are general government.

Financial and budgetary rules regulating different levels of government allowed for some slack in financial discipline. For example, there were no controls on, nor systematic accounting of, arrears accu-mulated by the CBIs. Until 1995, the SSFs had un-limited access to the current account of the State Budget at the National Bank of Hungary. At the same time, the SSFs did not always bear responsibility for

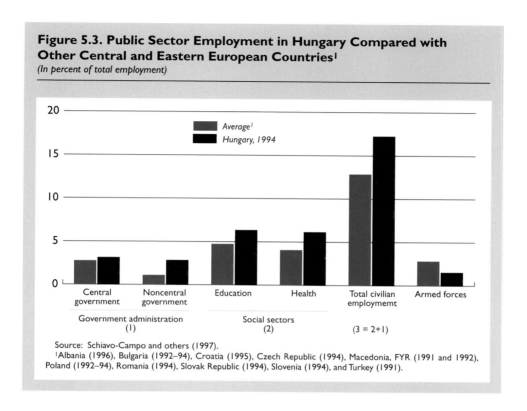

Figure 5.3. Public Sector Employment in Hungary Compared with Other Central and Eastern European Countries[1]
(In percent of total employment)

Source: Schiavo-Campo and others (1997).
[1]Albania (1996), Bulgaria (1992–94), Croatia (1995), Czech Republic (1994), Macedonia, FYR (1991 and 1992), Poland (1992–94), Romania (1994), Slovak Republic (1994), Slovenia (1994), and Turkey (1991).

their deficits. For example, in 1996, the budget of the Health Insurance Fund (HIF) was prepared under the assumptions of large savings from the closure of hospital beds and new pharmaceutical legislation. None of these measures materialized in time nor bore their budgeted yield. One consequence of the complex institutional structure and of the lack of information systems was that budgets tended to be formulated incrementally, rather than being based on a comprehensive review of expenditure priorities (OECD, 1995a).

The Pension System

The structure of the Hungarian social expenditure system in the early 1990s was essentially intact from the former period, and it was characterized by untargeted social benefits, lax eligibility conditions for old age, survivors, and disability pensions, and generalized access to health care. The job losses generated by the economic transformation were absorbed through a sharp rise in early retirement, particularly disability, and disguised unemployment (Chapter X).[5] The result was a social protection system with high access, low benefits, and high social security contributions.

The financial pressures on the pension system have been directly related to the policies prevailing during Hungary's transition to a market economy, rather than to population aging. The dependency ratio (the ratio of pensioners to workers—36 percent in 1995) has been high and rising during the 1990s due to (1) a reduction in the labor force participation rate (which fell from 85 percent to 76 percent between 1990 and 1994); (2) the increase in registered unemployment (which rose from 0.3 percent in 1990 to about 10 percent in 1995); and (3) an increase in the rate of early retirement, partly due to ad-hoc publicly financed schemes (OECD, 1995b), and of disability pensions (whose number increased by 32 percent between January 1990 and January 1995—Figure 5.4). By 1995, there was almost one disabled person for each 10 healthy Hungarians above age 15. Moreover, contribution revenue declined significantly, from 11 percent of GDP in 1991 to 8.9 percent of GDP in 1995,[6] mainly owing to a reduction of the formal sector wage bill relative to total labor income (in turn owing to a shift of workers to self-employment status to minimize overall tax liabilities) and

---

[5]In 1994, about 600,000 unemployed, though statistically counted as employed, were sheltered in various long-term leave and work/training programs (World Bank, 1995).

[6]These are the contributions revenue to finance old age, survivors, and disability pensions. Contribution revenue for the two SSFs together declined from 16.9 percent of GDP in 1990 to 13.3 percent of GDP in 1995. The decline in 1995 is also due to the wage policies of the March stabilization package, as real average wages fell by more than 10 percent in that year.

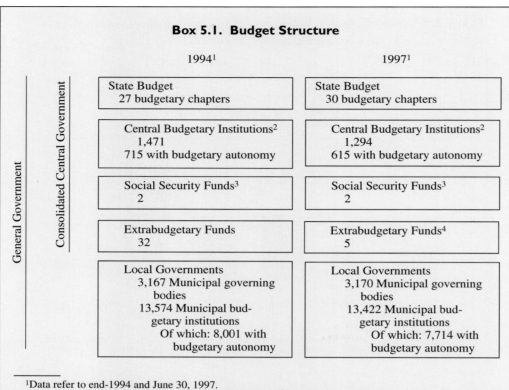

Box 5.1. Budget Structure

		1994[1]	1997[1]
General Government	Consolidated Central Government	**State Budget** 27 budgetary chapters	**State Budget** 30 budgetary chapters
		Central Budgetary Institutions[2] 1,471 715 with budgetary autonomy	**Central Budgetary Institutions[2]** 1,294 615 with budgetary autonomy
		Social Security Funds[3] 2	**Social Security Funds[3]** 2
		Extrabudgetary Funds 32	**Extrabudgetary Funds[4]** 5
		Local Governments 3,167 Municipal governing bodies 13,574 Municipal budgetary institutions Of which: 8,001 with budgetary autonomy	**Local Governments** 3,170 Municipal governing bodies 13,422 Municipal budgetary institutions Of which: 7,714 with budgetary autonomy

[1]Data refer to end-1994 and June 30, 1997.

[2]The Central Budgetary Institutions are the decentralized spending units of the ministries. Those with budgetary autonomy have the authority to raise own nontax revenue.

[3]The two social security funds are the Pension Insurance Fund and the Health Insurance Fund.

[4]The five extrabudgetary funds operating in 1997 are the Road Fund (managed by the Ministry of Transportation), the Employment Fund (managed by the Ministry of Labor), the National Culture Fund (managed by the Ministry of Education and Culture), the Water Management Fund (managed by the Ministry of Transportation), and the Environment Protection Fund (managed by the Ministry for Environment).

of the labor income share in GDP (in turn owing to falling labor force participation rates and increasing unemployment) (Palacios and Rocha, 1997).

The deficit of the Pension Insurance Fund (PIF) would have skyrocketed under the impact of the above factors had it not been for the fall in the average replacement ratio (ratio of average pension to average wage). This fall was due to three factors: (1) less than full actualization of past contributions; (2) lack of adjustment of the wage brackets in the benefit formula (leading to a reverse bracket creeping effect); and (3) indexation of pensions to the expected net average wage during the upcoming calendar year. As a result, the real value of the average pension declined by 13.1 percent between 1990 and 1994.

The Health Care System

The problems of the Hungarian health system do not relate to the level of public expenditure for health care. Total public health expenditure varied

between 6.5 percent of GDP and 7.4 percent of GDP during 1991–94, and then declined to 6.3 percent of GDP in 1996. This level of public health expenditures is not large for Hungary's level of economic development—as measured by the level of GDP per capita—in comparison with both the OECD countries and other transition economies (Figure 5.5).

The main problems of the Hungarian health care system are its low efficiency, as measured in terms of capacity and input indicators and health outcomes, and the size and unpredictability of the deficit of the HIF. The supply of health care services is characterized by excessive reliance on inpatient care and, in particular, expensive acute care, low ratio of nurses to doctors, and high use of specialist services. This is in large part the legacy of the prereform system, when health sector performance was measured principally in terms of quantitative indicators, such as the number of doctors and hospital beds, rather than performance indicators. In terms of health outcomes, the health status of the Hungarian population, as measured by life

Figure 5.4. Disability Pensions

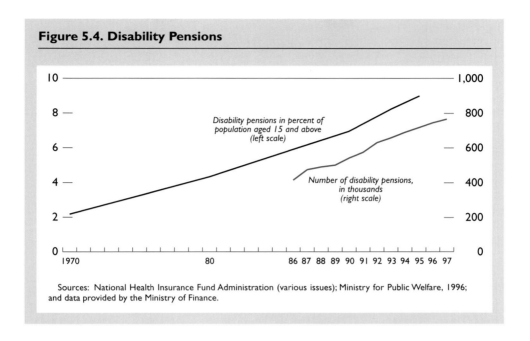

Disability pensions in percent of population aged 15 and above (left scale)

Number of disability pensions, in thousands (right scale)

1970   80   86 87 88 89 90 91 92 93 94 95 96 97

Sources: National Health Insurance Fund Administration (various issues); Ministry for Public Welfare, 1996; and data provided by the Ministry of Finance.

expectancy at birth, is by far the lowest among OECD countries and one of the lowest among the central European countries in transition (Figure 5.6). This was not the case before the mid-1970s. The life expectancy of Hungarian males is now two years lower than in 1970–75; the life expectancy of women has increased, but not at the same pace as in other European countries. The main causes of death in Hungary are related to lifestyle (i.e., smoking, alcohol consumption, and dietary habits) (Józan, 1996), rather than to the level of efficiency of the health care system. However, its lack of effectiveness, and its low ability to adapt to demographic and epidemiological changes, have stimulated public debate.

The deficits of the HIF have consistently overshot their target—usually set at, or close to, zero percent of GDP (Figure 5.7). As discussed above, the divergence between the approved budget and the outcome is due both to nonimplementation of approved measures and to optimistic assumptions regarding yields from measures. Though the deficit is small in comparison to GDP, it is large when compared to total revenue of the HIF—it has ranged between 5 percent and 9 percent of HIF revenue from 1994 to 1997. The "unpredictability" of the HIF deficit has reinforced concerns regarding the efficient management of health expenditures.

Subsidies and Central Budget Social Transfers

A significant portion of the Hungarian consolidated central budget expenditures is devoted to subsidies to (1) different industries; (2) agriculture (including for exports); (3) consumers; and (4) pharmaceuticals. These four types of subsidies accounted for 4½ per-

cent of GDP in 1994.[7] The central budget disburses other social transfers, most notably family and child allowances and housing subsidies. These accounted for 4½ percent of GDP and 0.7 percent of GDP, respectively, in 1994. Most subsidies and the social transfers were untargeted and open-ended (actual expenditures at the end of the year were ultimately determined not by the budgetary allocation, but by the number of claimants satisfying the eligibility conditions). Lack of targeting resulted in an inefficient use of public outlays. This was the case for both social expenditures—when the nonpoor receive social transfers and subsidies—and industrial and agricultural subsidies—when the nature of subsidies is such that it actually hinders, rather than promotes, efficient allocation of production and economic transformation. The open-endedness of subsidy and social transfers resulted in unpredictability of public expenditures. Commitments during the year were often higher than budgetary allocations, and would eventually be accommodated in revised budgets.

Smaller Deficit, Smaller Government

In 1995, the Council of Ministers approved a public finance reform program, where it laid out a strategic plan for reforming the role of the public sector in the

[7]These are the explicit subsidies in the budget only. In fact, other expenditure categories (i.e., investments) include outlays that should instead be classified as subsidies (i.e., transfers to households to reduce the interest costs of housing loans).

economy. Its final objective was to achieve a smaller, but more efficient general government, while at the same time strengthening the overall fiscal balance. The plan was structured along four fundamental lines: first, reforming social insurance; second, reducing the tax burden and improving tax administration; third, improving the management of public finances and restructuring public administration; and fourth, reforming intergovernmental finances. All structural changes intervened in the mid-1990s in the area of public finance fit in these four broad categories.

Many of the trends in revenues and expenditures during 1994–97 (which are discussed in the next section) can be interpreted in light of the above strategy. However, these trends are not the result of major

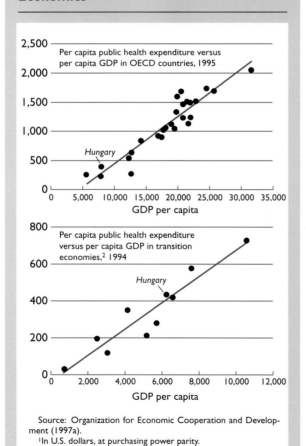

Figure 5.5. Per Capita Public Health Expenditures Versus Per Capita GDP in OECD Countries and Selected Transition Economies[1]

Source: Organization for Economic Cooperation and Development (1997a).

[1]In U.S. dollars, at purchasing power parity.

[2]Countries include Hungary, Albania, Bulgaria, Croatia, Czech Republic (1993), Poland (1993), Macedonia, FYR (1993), Romania, Slovak Republic, and Slovenia.

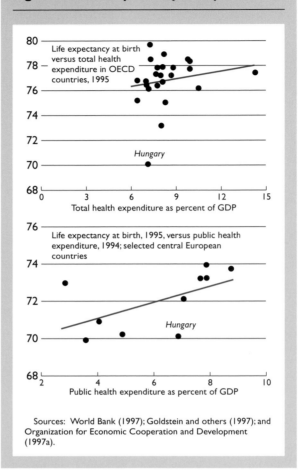

Figure 5.6. Life Expectancy Comparisons

Sources: World Bank (1997); Goldstein and others (1997); and Organization for Economic Cooperation and Development (1997a).

structural reforms, but of what could be described as "the silent reform": several policy measures in different areas that nevertheless considerably furthered the implementation of the overall strategy outlined by the government in 1995. Structural reforms were also approved (mainly old age pensions, health care, and treasury; see below), but their effect will materialize primarily in the medium term.

At the aggregate level, the most apparent results achieved during 1994–97 are the strengthening in the primary balance of the consolidated central government and the dramatic fall in expenditure and revenue ratios. The primary revenue-to-GDP ratio—excluding privatization proceeds—and the primary expenditure-to-GDP ratios dropped, respectively, by 8.3 percentage points and 13.2 percentage points (Figure 5.1).[8]

---

[8]In this chapter, all revenues and expenditure ratios for 1997 refer to the 1997 budget, as a detailed breakdown of actual revenues and expenditures is not yet available.

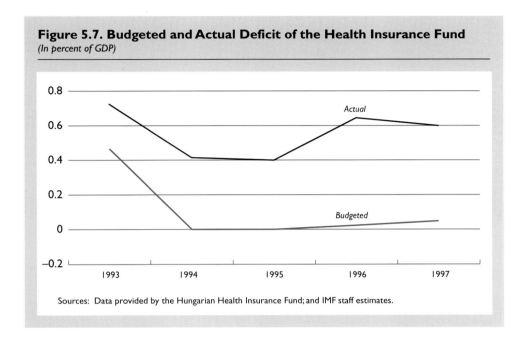

Figure 5.7. Budgeted and Actual Deficit of the Health Insurance Fund
(In percent of GDP)

Sources: Data provided by the Hungarian Health Insurance Fund; and IMF staff estimates.

As a result, the primary balance improved by 4.8 percentage points of GDP (Table 5.1). About one-half of this improvement was achieved in 1995. In this year alone, the government accomplished 61 percent and 59 percent, respectively, of the total adjustment in primary expenditures and in revenue achieved over 1994–97.[9]

Part of the decline (about 2 percentage points of GDP) was due to institutional changes, rather than to cuts in underlying public expenditure and revenue. Within the framework of reforming the government role in the economy, 17 CBIs, and networks of CBIs, were transformed into economic associations or nonprofit organizations and left the budget sphere during 1994–97. The removal of these institutions—which continue to perform their public role (mainly supervision and quality control of specific economic sectors, management of state property, and public media)—from the central government definition

lowered revenues and expenditure ratios by 1.5 percent of GDP over 1994–97. Moreover, the share of the Personal Income Tax (PIT) accruing to local governments (LGs) was raised, with an offsetting cut in transfers from the central government. This accounts for another drop by 0.3–0.4 percent of GDP in revenues and expenditure ratios. It is also possible that the reorganization of EBFs may have led to a decline in own revenues and expenditures of these institutions, although this effect is more difficult to quantify.

Decline in Primary Expenditures

Primary expenditures were cut in real terms across the board (Table 5.1). The only outlays that remained immune from cutbacks were already at modest levels in 1994: consumer subsidies and central budget investments. The expenditure categories that fell in real terms more than the average reduction in expenses have been those where some structural steps were taken: industrial and agricultural subsidies, transfers to local governments, family allowances and other income supplement benefits, sickness payments, and maternity allowances. However, other outlays (such as wages and disability and old age pensions) also dropped drastically in real terms, reflecting tight budgetary nominal allocations in the presence of high inflation (particularly in 1995). In the remaining part of this section, we will review the main reasons behind the reduction in the above-mentioned expenditure categories.

---

[9]The 1995 adjustment reflected primarily the package approved in March 1995, the so-called Bokros package, named after the Minister of Finance who put it forward. The main elements of this package were, on the revenue side: the imposition of a temporary 8 percent import surcharge (with the exception of energy and machinery imports); excise tax increases, particularly on cars; and an expansion of the social security contribution base. Revenues were also aided by higher inflation and devaluation (Chapter II). On the expenditure side, the package included: (1) a cut in wage allocations to CBIs by a further 3 percent; (2) a freeze of current purchases in nominal terms; and (3) amendments to public sector employment laws so as to facilitate employment cuts. The proposed replacement of universal family and child allowances with targeted social assistance was cancelled by the Constitutional Court—and approved in 1996, in a different form.

Table 5.1. Budget of Consolidated Central Government

	1994	1995	1996	Budget 1997	Change 1994–97	Real Change
			(In percent of GDP)			
Revenues	49.1	45.9	47.3	42.2	6.9	0.84
Primary revenue[1]	48.2	45.3	45.7	39.8	−8.4	0.80
Primary revenue excluding privatization revenue	47.5	42.6	42.4	39.2	−8.3	0.77
Taxes on profits and income	7.5	7.1	7.8	6.8	−0.7	0.88
Social security contributions	17.1	14.4	13.7	14.4	−2.8	0.82
VAT	7.7	7.6	7.7	7.9	0.2	1.00
Excises	3.8	3.6	3.3	3.4	−0.4	0.87
Custom duties	3.4	4.5	3.7	2.5	−0.9	0.70
Privatization	0.7	2.7	3.3	0.6	−0.1	0.86
Interest revenue + National Bank of Hungary payments	0.9	0.6	1.7	2.4	1.5	2.65
Other revenue	8.0	5.5	6.1	4.3	−3.7	0.53
CBIs own revenue	3.8	2.8	3.0	1.6	−2.3	0.40
EBFs own revenue	2.5	1.4	1.2	1.1	−1.4	0.43
Other revenue	1.7	1.2	1.9	1.7	0.0	0.98
Expenditures	55.5	49.6	47.2	46.4	−9.0	0.81
Primary expenditure[2]	48.8	40.7	37.9	35.6	−13.2	0.71
Subsidies	4.5	3.8	3.9	3.3	−1.2	0.71
CB industrial/agricultural subsidies	2.3	1.7	1.7	1.4	−0.9	0.59
Consumer subsidies	0.6	0.6	0.7	0.6	0.0	0.99
SSFs pharmaceutical subsidies	1.6	1.5	1.5	1.3	−0.3	0.78
Transfers to local government	6.8	5.8	4.9	4.6	−2.3	0.65
Social transfers	17.7	15.5	14.1	13.3	−4.3	0.73
Family allowances	4.8	3.7	3.2	2.6	−2.2	0.53
Old-age pensions	8.8	8.0	7.6	7.7	−1.1	0.85
Disability pensions	1.3	1.2	1.2	1.2	−0.2	0.85
Sickness payments	0.9	0.7	0.5	0.5	−0.4	0.52
Maternity allowances	0.2	0.2	0.1	0.1	−0.1	0.51
Unemployment benefits	0.9	0.7	0.8	0.8	−0.1	0.88
Housing subsidies	0.7	1.1	0.8	0.5	−0.2	0.66
Wages (CBIs + SSFs)	3.9	3.6	3.2	3.2	−0.7	0.79
CB investment expenditure	1.0	0.9	1.0	1.2	0.2	1.13
CBIs own expenditure	4.3	2.6	2.8	1.3	−3.0	0.30
EBFs own expenditure	3.9	2.3	1.7	1.7	−2.2	0.42
Other expenditures	6.6	6.3	6.3	10.0	3.4	1.47
Interest payments + transfers to National Bank of Hungary	6.7	8.9	9.3	10.9	4.2	1.58
Consolidated deficit	−6.4	−3.7	0.1	−4.3	2.2	...
Excluding privatization revenue	−7.1	−6.4	−3.2	−4.9	2.2	...
Primary balance[1]	−0.6	4.6	7.7	4.1	4.7	...
(Excluding privatization revenue)	−1.3	1.9	4.4	3.5	4.8	...

Sources: Ministry of Finance; and IMF staff estimates.

[1]Primary revenue is defined as total revenue minus interest revenues and transfer of profits from the National Bank of Hungary.

[2]Primary expenditure is defined as total expenditure minus interest payments and transfers to cover the losses of the National Bank of Hungary.

An important contribution to the decline in the primary deficit over 1994–97 came from the cut by almost 1 percentage point of GDP in agricultural and industrial subsidies, as a result of a tightening in eligibility conditions. Agricultural subsidies had overrun budget estimates by about 30 percent in 1994. The cost overrun was most pronounced for export subsidies, which were volume specific, and therefore, there was no control on outlays. In 1995, the subsidy was specified in terms of export value in dollars. However, reflecting the March 1995 devaluation, this new system also led to higher-than-expected expenditures. To eliminate this problem, since 1996, the per-unit export subsidy has been denominated in forint. In 1997, the list of subsidized products was shortened, the average per-unit subsidy

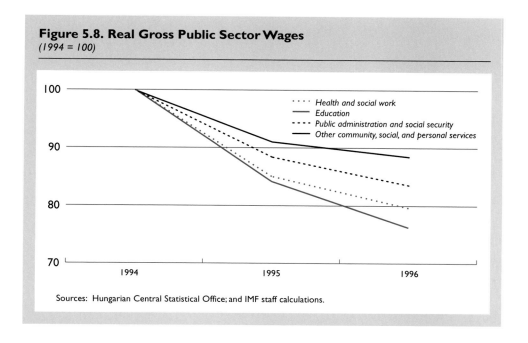

Figure 5.8. Real Gross Public Sector Wages
(1994 = 100)

Health and social work
Education
Public administration and social security
Other community, social, and personal services

Sources: Hungarian Central Statistical Office; and IMF staff calculations.

in forint was cut, and product specific ceilings on the exported quantities eligible for subsidies were introduced. The latter measure, together with the imposition of expenditure ceilings and application deadlines on domestic agricultural and industrial subsidies, effectively eliminated the open-endedness character of the explicit subsidies to economic units.

In line with the long-term policy to decentralize the responsibility for financing local services, the central budget has gradually reduced its transfers to LGs, another key component of the adjustment.[10] This reduction helped in forcing LGs to cut their expenditure by 3 percent of GDP during 1994–97,[11] and to increase their own revenues.[12]

---

[10]After the establishment of a two-tier system of government in 1990–91, the delivery of education, health, and social welfare services was devolved to LGs with the objective of making the provision of these services more responsive to local demand, and strengthening accountability of local administrators. As noted above, a small part of the reduction in transfers was offset by a larger allocation to LGs of PIT revenues. The PIT transferred to the LGs is assigned partly on a derivation basis (to the same municipality on whose territory it is collected) and partly on an equalization basis (to poorer municipalities). The latter portion has increased over the last few years, and it will continue to do so until the year 2000, when it will reach 20 percent of the PIT collection—out of a total of 40 percent transferred to LGs.

[11]Employment in LGs was reduced by 7 percent to about 533,000 people in 1997.

[12]The percentage of own current revenue in total revenue increased by 2.8 percentage points to about 20 percent. Shared revenue increased by 5 percent to about 14 percent, and transfers decreased by 6.5 percent to about 36 percent.

The third major component of the adjustment in expenditure was the cut in family allowances and other targeted social assistance subsidies, which declined by 2.2 percentage points of GDP to 2.7 percent—a decline of about 45 percent in real terms. This fall was due to two reasons. First—as for other social benefits, including pensions—nominal benefits have not kept pace with inflation. Second, entitlement conditions to family and child allowances have been redesigned to improve targeting. As of April 1996, eligibility to family allowance for the first two children was made conditional on an income test. Other children-related allowances were either eliminated or became conditional to an income test.

Sickness payments were cut by 68 percent in real terms. In 1994, sickness payments had generous replacement rates of 65–75 percent of net earnings and could last up to one year. They were also widely abused. The key policy issue here was the number of days to be paid by the employer, as this affected the incentive for the employer to control abuse. Starting in 1995, employers paid the first 10 days of sick leave, and these were increased to 15 in 1996.

The wage bill of CBIs and SSFs fell by 0.7 percentage points of GDP, reflecting cuts in real wages and employment (which did not affect all sectors equally; Figure 5.8). These cuts were concentrated in 1995 and 1996, and real wages have increased already in 1997.

Similar trends arise for pensions expenditure. Real per-capita pensions, which had already declined significantly during 1990–94 (see above), fell by an ad-

---

Box 5.2. Main Tax Measures, 1994–97[1]

Introduced with the 1995 Budget

- The *VAT* base is broadened and rates are increased. Selected pharmaceutical products start being taxed at 12 percent, and the rates on telecommunications and household fuel are changed from 10 percent to 25 percent. The 10 percent rate is changed to 12 percent. With these measures, the average effective tax rate moves closer to 25 percent (the rate at which most goods are taxed).

- *CIT* rates are defined differently. The single rate (36 percent) on company profits is replaced by a competitive (18 percent) rate at the corporate level and a supplementary tax of 33.3 percent on distributed profits. With this strategy, the government dismantles in practice most existing preferential tax treatments, although it also introduces an incentive for reinvestment of profits of questionable effectiveness. The withholding tax on dividends is reduced (in November, 1994) from 20 percent to 10 percent. The deductions, allowances, and other incentives previously available to reduce total taxable income are replaced by a tax credit system to broaden the taxable base. During 1995, a ceiling of 81.3 percent of profits is imposed on their distribution of profits. This measure was designed to limit the tax avoidance by the owners of unincorporated businesses.[2]

- Several specific *excises* are increased.

- Most deductions from the *PIT* tax bases are transformed into tax credits. The withholding tax on dividends is reduced (in November, 1994) from 20 percent to 10 percent.

Introduced in the March 1995 Package

- An *import surcharge* of 8 percent until mid-1997 on all imports with the exception of energy and machinery.

- *Excise* tax increases, particularly on cars.

- Expansion of the *contribution base* for the health and pension funds.

Introduced with the 1996 Budget

- A new *PIT* schedule, including an increase of the top marginal rate from 44 percent to 48 percent, and broadening the base of assessment. A higher tax burden is imposed on persons having income from different sources (e.g., business income) through the application of a different PIT schedule.

- In *CIT*, stricter rules are applied regarding the deductibility of expenses and expenses incurred in connection with transactions whose primary purpose is tax avoidance, and new temporary industry-specific and regional tax incentives are introduced. In May 1996, the 1995 restrictions that had abolished, or restricted, incentives for foreign investors were declared unconstitutional with retroactive effect to January 1, 1995.

Introduced with the 1997 Budget

- The split-rate *CIT* structure is abolished and replaced by a single tax rate of 18 percent, which is one of the lowest in Europe. The dividend withholding tax is increased to a rate of 20 percent (27 percent on "excess" dividends); interest and royalties paid to nonresidents are subject to withholding tax at 18 percent under a "first pay then reclaim" system. The measures are designed to promote neutrality in competition and to take another step in harmonization with European standards.

- The *PIT* dual rate structure is again merged into a single one and the top rate reduced from 48 percent to 42 percent. The withholding tax on dividends is increased from 10 percent to 20 percent, and to 27 percent for "excess" dividends.

---

[1]Additionally, small changes to excise rates, particularly to specific excises, are implemented almost every year.

[2]These businesses were able to reduce their overall tax liability by taking out most of their income from their business in the form of dividend rather than wages (on which a high marginal PIT schedule and social contribution rates apply).

---

ditional 18 percent during 1995–96. However, already in 1997, average real pensions are projected to have increased by slightly less than 2 percent.

Decline in Primary Revenue

Most revenue fell in real terms, with the notable exception of VAT, and with relatively stronger declines for security contributions and custom duties (Table 5.1). As discussed above, a driving force behind the revenue decline was the government's attempt to reduce the tax burden to support growth and improve compliance (see section on tax administra-

tion). Unfortunately, many of these measures (which are listed in Box 5.2) also heightened the variability and complexity of tax regulations. The changes to tax policy have been too frequent and sometimes implemented without sufficient consultation. Indeed, some tax measures had to be withdrawn or substantially altered shortly after their introduction.

The decline in social insurance contributions by 2.7 percentage points of GDP is the result of several factors. First, a cut in rates (Table 5.2), which were high by international standards (Figure 5.9) and discouraged compliance (World Bank, 1995; OECD, 1995a). This accounts for a decline in contributions

Table 5.2. Social Insurance Contribution Rates
(In percent)

	1994	1995	1996	1997
Total contributions	60.8	60.0	58.5	55.0
Employer	49.3	48.5	47.0	43.5
Employee	11.5	11.5	11.5	11.5
Pension Fund	30.5	30.5	30.5	30.0
Employer	24.5	24.5	24.5	24.0
Employee	6.0	6.0	6.0	6.0
Health Insurance Fund	23.5	23.5	22.0	19.0
Employer	19.5	19.5	18.0	15.0
Employee	4.0	4.0	4.0	4.0
Labor Market Fund[1, 2]	6.8	6.0	6.0	6.0
Employer	5.3	4.5	4.5	4.5
Solidarity Fund	5.0	4.2	4.2	4.2
Wage Guarantee Fund	0.3	0.3	0.3	0.3
Employee	1.5	1.5	1.5	1.5

Sources: Ministry of Finance; and World Bank (1995).

[1]The Solidarity Fund and the Wage Guarantee Fund were merged into the Labor Market Fund in 1996.

[2]Excludes the Rehabilitation Contribution. This is paid by employers, employing more than 20 people, that are not employing disabled workers for at least 5 percent of staff. The contribution in 1997 was Ft 8,000*(5−x), where x is percentage of disabled staff.

by 1.8 percentage points of GDP. Second, the shift in income distribution: wages and salaries, as a percent of GDP, declined from 36.1 percent in 1994 to 32.7 percent in 1997. Had the wage share in GDP not changed, contributions would have been 1.5 percentage points of GDP higher. These two effects were offset by the broadening of the contribution base (primarily through the inclusion of fringe benefits) and by closing some tax loopholes (most important, those related to income from intellectual income, and business income from nonincorporated partnership).[13] Moreover, in 1997, a minimum tax of Ft 1,800 was imposed on all citizens for access to curative health services, and the ceiling on workers' wage subject contribution payment was increased.

The sharp fall in customs revenues was almost entirely driven by tariff reductions due to the Hungar-

[13]There are no social security contributions payable on business income from nonincorporated partnerships. Therefore, to avoid paying high social security contributions, entrepreneurs fired workers and rehired them on contracts. These workers would then set up partnerships from which they would receive substantial revenue in forms of dividends. As a result, there were about 100,000 nonincorporated partnerships in 1996. These tax regulations not only erode the base of the social security contribution, but also reduced PIT revenue. In 1997, to alleviate this problem, a higher rate on the PIT withholding tax on capital income was imposed on the distribution of "excess" dividends.

ian government commitments to the Association Agreement with the European Union and to the World Trade Organization (WTO). During 1994–97, the effective rate of custom duty—the ratio of duty revenue, including statistical fees, to dutiable imports—declined from 9½ percent to about 3½ percent. This cut was initially offset by the import surcharge (see above and Chapter IX), which was gradually reduced and fully eliminated at mid-1997.

Other revenue items posting large reductions are from the own revenue of the CBIs and of the EBFs (Table 5.1). As discussed above, three-fourths of the fall in CBIs' own revenue is due to the removal of some CBIs from the budgetary sphere. The decline in EBFs' own revenue may, at least in part, reflect the reorganization of the sector and the elimination of financial flows with other branches of the general government. The EBFs had independent revenue sources, including from commercial activities, and independent spending authority. Between 1995 and 1997, the government wound down most funds by merging some of them or by absorbing them in the ministries from which they depended. As a result, the number of EBFs fell from 32 to 5 (Box 5.1). Moreover, their budgetary independence has been curtailed, and they were brought into the treasury system in 1996, with positive effects on cash management for the consolidated central government (see below).

More than one-half of the fall in PIT revenue is due to the above-mentioned increase of the PIT share going to the LGs. However, other factors have been at play (Table 5.3). First, in 1995, the fall in real wages reduced the tax base by 3.4 percentage points of GDP. Second, bracket creeping had an enhancing effect on PIT revenue, as the effective tax rate increased by 9.4 percentage points of the tax base between 1994 and 1997—notwithstanding the reduction in the rate schedule implemented in 1997. Third, the importance of tax credits has continuously increased, as they now reduce retained revenue by 2.5 percentage points of GDP. As a result of these offsetting forces, the net effective tax rate has been remarkably stable during 1994–97.

As to other taxes, the decline in excises is mainly due to the fact that consumption—which is closely related to excise taxation—has declined from 85 percent of GDP to 76 percent of GDP during 1994–97 (the ratio of excise revenue to consumption has remained broadly stable over the period). Corporate Income Tax (CIT) revenue has decreased only marginally, despite an increase in the taxable profits by 3.8 percentage points of GDP over 1994–95. This fall in revenue is due to the halving of the CIT rate from 36 percent in 1994 to 18 percent in 1997. The increase in VAT revenue is due mainly to base broadening and the elimination of exemptions implemented in 1995

Figure 5.9. Contribution Rates for Social Security Programs in Hungary and Selected OECD Countries[1]

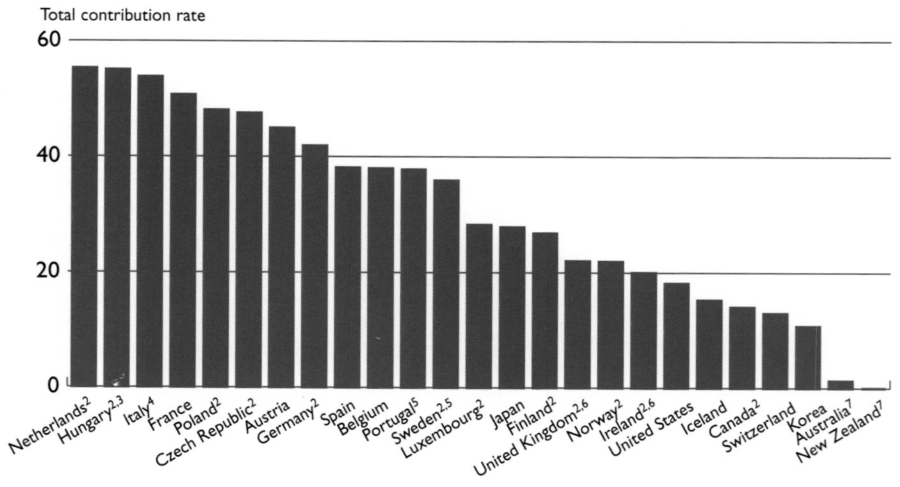

Total contribution rate

Source: U.S. Social Security Administration (1997).
[1]Includes Old Age, Disability, Death; Sickness and Maternity; Work Injury; Unemployment; and Family Allowances. In some countries, the rate may not cover all of these programs. In some cases, only certain groups, such as wage earners, are represented.
[2]The central government pays the whole cost of Family Allowances.
[3]Plus flat amount for disability (see Table 5.3).
[4]Plus flat amount for Work Injury.
[5]Plus flat amount for Unemployment.
[6]Range according to earnings bracket. Higher rate is shown, which applies to highest earnings class.
[7]The central government pays the entire cost of most programs from general revenues.

and to administrative improvements, which were particularly relevant in 1997 (see next section).

Structural Reforms

Structural reforms have been implemented in four main areas: (1) the institutional structure; (2) the pension system; (3) the health care system; and (4) tax and customs administration.

Institutional Structure

Important structural changes were implemented in this area. The treasury started operating on January 1, 1996. All cash money from central government agencies and institutions started passing through a single treasury account held at the National Bank of Hungary, thus replacing a multitude of previously existing accounts. This allowed the central government to keep track of, and optimize the use of, cash balances held by its entities. The treasury was also assigned the supervision of the disbursement of subsidies to enterprises and of

transfers to other entities of the general government. This allowed the implementation of a system of net financing for LGs: the treasury started transferring the LGs' PIT share after netting it out of social security contributions due by LGs to SSFs and EBFs. The same has occurred for subsidies to enterprises: the treasury does not effect any transfer to organizations that have social security or tax arrears. These changes have improved collection rates for social security and tax revenue. In April 1996, the Center for Government Debt Management also came under the authority of the treasury. In January 1997, also the accounts of the SSFs were brought into the treasury system. At the same time, the treasury started recording commitments against budgetary appropriations and payments for CBIs' expenditures regulated by the new Public Procurement Law, thus allowing a better monitoring of arrears. The Public Procurement Law itself introduced transparency and major economies in purchases by both the central and local governments.

The establishment of the treasury has made available real-time information on the cash and debt posi-

Table 5.3. PIT Indicators

	1994	1995	1996	1997
	(In percent of GDP)			
Progressive tax base	34.6	31.2	31.8	29.4
Net of deductions	30.2	31.2	31.8	29.4
	(In percent of tax base)			
Effective tax rate[1]	20.0	26.2	31.8	29.4
Net effective tax rate[2]	21.5	21.3	23.1	21.5
	(In percent of GDP)			
Memorandum item:				
Tax credits	0.4	1.5	2.3	2.5

Sources: Ministry of Finance; and IMF staff estimates.

[1]Ratio of PIT collections (on progressive schedule only) to net progressive tax base.

[2]Ratio of PIT collections (on progressive schedule only) minus tax credits to net progressive tax base.

tion, expenditure disbursed, and revenue collected of all entities of the consolidated central government. However, this centralization of accounts was not accompanied by changes in budgetary codes and by a new chart of accounts. Therefore, it remains difficult to classify government operations according to full economic and functional lines.

New budgeting, accounting, and reporting rules were introduced for the SSFs in 1996. The SSF budgets are now formulated within the time frame of the overall government budget. These changes have eliminated the possibility of delays in approving the budgets of the SSFs, which were all too common in the past. The SSFs are now also required to present quarterly budgetary reports to Parliament and to the government, and to prepare long-term projections of their revenue and expenditures. Since December 1996, the General Assembly of the SSFs has lost its veto power on government decrees related to social insurance. Finally, a new institutional law was adopted by Parliament in June 1997, reforming the procedures of nomination of members to the General Assembly of the Self-Governments.

Pension Reform

The pension reform has been approved in two parts. First, in 1996, the existing pay-as-you-go (PAYG) system was reformed. Second, in 1997, a new multipillar pension system, including a fully funded component, was established for implementation in January 1998. Hungary is the first country in Eastern Europe to adopt a multipillar pension system, and the second country in Europe (after the United Kingdom) to make a switch to a multipillar system.

The most significant changes to the existing PAYG were (1) a gradual increase in retirement age (combined with a rise in the minimum years of service for early retirement); (2) the shift from wage indexation of pensions to a combination of wages and prices with equal weights; (3) the introduction of a new benefit formula; (4) tighter eligibility criteria; (5) changes in the rules regarding survivors' benefits; and (6) changes in the tax treatment of pension benefits and contributions (Box 5.3). The first two measures have the strongest positive impact on the finances of the system. The other measures have a lesser fiscal impact, but have important implications for the incentives to comply and for income distribution.

The multipillar system comprises a new and downsized first pillar—publicly managed and financed on a PAYG basis—and a new second pillar—privately managed and fully funded. A voluntary third pillar (also privately managed and fully funded) has been in operation since early 1994.[14] The new system will be mandatory for all new entrants into the labor force as of July 1, 1998. Workers who have entered the labor market before July 1998 will have the option of staying in the reformed PAYG or to switch to the new system. Workers staying in the reformed PAYG could expect an entry pension, before taxes, of 60–65 percent of the average wage. Workers under 35–40 years of age are likely to find it attractive to shift to the new system, as below this age, the expected return on the second pillar accounts will outweigh the partial loss of benefits accrued under the old system, leading to an entry level pension of 65–72 percent of the average wage.

The flow of resources to the second pillar and, therefore, its impact on the deficit of the PIF would average 1 percent of GDP in the first years of implementation.[15] After 10 years of implementation, the assets accumulated in second pillar accounts could amount to approximately 15 percent of GDP.[16] There

[14]By mid-1997, the number of contributors to the third pillar had reached 575,000, or roughly 15 percent of the labor force.

[15]An additional fiscal cost of the transition is a new PIT credit of 25 percent of employee contribution to the first and second pillar. The impact of this credit on PIT revenue is likely to be about 0.5 percent of GDP.

[16]The private pension funds managing these assets would be legally structured along the lines of the private pension funds already operating since early 1994, called voluntary mutual benefit funds. However, the regulatory framework for the second pillar will be stricter than the framework currently guiding the voluntary third pillar. In particular, pension funds operating in the second pillar will be subject to a minimum size, contribute to a central Guarantee Fund, hire custodian services, submit quarterly reports to the supervision agency, subject to some investment guidelines, and subject to stricter professional requirements for asset management.

Box 5.3. Reform of the PAYG and New First Pillar

Retirement Age Increase

The statutory retirement age will gradually reach age 62 by the year 2009. Until that year, workers have the option of retiring as early as age 57 without penalty if they have completed the required number of statutory years of participation in the system. Retirement with fewer years of service is also possible but with a penalty. After 2009, the earliest a person can retire is age 59 if the worker has completed 37 years of service. Those who have accumulated 40 years of service can retire between ages 59 and 62 without any penalty. The changes in retirement age regulations are expected to lead to an increase in the effective retirement age of approximately 5–6 years for women and 2–2½ years for men by the year 2010.

Indexation Rules

The change in indexation involves a gradual shift from annual net wage indexation to an evenly weighted average to wages and prices. The net wage indexation will be maintained in 1998 and 1999 to allow a partial compensation for the decline in real pensions in 1995 and 1996, the years when real pensions declined significantly. In 2000, the government will start delinking pensions from wages, applying a mixed formula of 30 percent price and 70 percent net wage indexation. The 50/50 indexation formula will be fully implemented in 2000. Under the assumption that GDP and real wage growth will average 3–4 percent a year in the next decade, the reforms would lead the PAYG generating surpluses of more than 1.5 percent of GDP during that period—before the losses associated with the introduction of the second pillar are taken into account.

Benefit Formula

The new benefit formula applies a set of lower coefficients to a worker's *gross* wage history. The new formula will be used for the calculation of new pensions after 2012, and will replace the current schedule of higher coefficients that are applied to a worker's *net* wages.

Eligibility Criteria

The number of noncontributory years counted toward retirement for students and women on maternity leave will be reduced.

Rules on Survivor Benefits

Starting in 1998, survivor pensions will be awarded regardless of other pension income. This change is applied retroactively and is estimated to add approximately 20 percent to the average survivor pension. However, since survivor benefits are low and account for a small share of pension expenditures, the increase in pension outlays generated by this change is expected to account for about 0.1 percent of GDP.

Taxation Treatment of Contributions and Benefits

The changes in the tax treatment include the introduction of a 25 percent tax credit on mandatory employee contributions (to the PAYG and the second pillar), exempting investment income in the second pillar and taxing pension benefits. Although the changes in the tax treatment imply a loss of revenues of the personal income tax of approximately 0.5 percent of GDP in the first stages of the reform, they move Hungary much closer to the tax treatment applied in most OECD countries, which involves exempting contributions and investment income while taxing benefits.

---

is a guarantee on minimum second pillar replacement rate defined as 25 percent of the replacement rate that the worker would receive from the first pillar. This guarantee effectively establishes a contingent liability for the new pension system, which has not been quantified yet. This liability is backed by resources of the Guarantee Fund. Mostly older workers, who have a shorter period of service, are likely to benefit from this guarantee. Therefore, the government expects this guarantee not to be large.[17]

The pension reform represents a key step forward in consolidating public finances in Hungary. The reform of the PAYG system goes a long way to reverse the otherwise inevitable deterioration of pension accounts in the long term.[18] Moreover, the introduction of a fully funded component is important in encouraging compliance and in developing the capital market. Other steps are expected to follow soon. A key issue that still needs to be addressed is disability pension reform. Although a parliamentary resolution adopted in July 1997 outlines its main principle and sets 1999 as the date for its implementation, much preparatory work needs to be done to meet this target.[19]

---

[17]The guarantee creates two additional problems. First, more people may decide to switch to the new system and, therefore, the costs of the transition may be higher. Second, the individual-specific guarantee may add to administrative costs, especially if the guarantee is frequently monitored by actuaries.

[18]The PAYG system is expected to remain in surplus for the next 30–35 years. Later, a deficit is expected to emerge, reflecting demographic trends.

[19]In the new system, vocational criteria—together with the current medical ones—will be used to determine eligibility as well as the degree of disability. Instead of focusing on the worker's lost ability to work, the new system will emphasize the worker's remaining ability to work. Permanent benefits will be awarded only to the most serious medical cases. The reform will require

Health Reform

It is misleading to say that the government implemented a full-fledged health reform in 1994–97. From the early 1990s, the government had already implemented a myriad of changes to the financing, delivery, and institutional structure of the health care system and it has continued to do so. Although over the past two years the legislative effort in this area has intensified, measures taken have fallen short of a fully fledged reform.

During the first half of the 1990s, Hungary moved from a centrally planned public health care system, financed through general budget revenues, to a delegated and decentralized system, financed through a combination of social insurance payments (to cover part of the outlays of the HIF), general budgetary revenue (for the outlays of the state and LGs), and patients' outlays for drugs and private medicine (Box 5.4). However, as discussed above, there are still numerous concerns regarding the efficiency of the system and its deficits.

In 1995, the government added to its legislative agenda the improvement of the efficiency of health care delivery and the reduction of its fiscal burden. This led to the approval of the Act on Capacity Reduction in July 1996,[20] the Act on Health Insurance in July 1997,[21] and the Act on Social Insurance Eligibility and Financing, regulating the revenue of both the PIF and HIF, also in July 1997. Moreover, the government presented to Parliament a draft of the Health Care Act, regulating the organization of the health sector.

A full discussion of these measures is included in Ruggiero (1997). Here, it is enough to note that the approved laws represent a useful streamlining of existing regulations and contain some useful measures. However, they fall short of introducing those economic incentives to efficiency that in the medium to long term will be necessary to improve the overall effectiveness and viability of the health system.[22] Moreover, in some cases (such as the Health Care Act), the new legislation provides a framework—outlining the basic principles regarding the role of the government, the rights and responsibilities of individuals, the agents/units included in the health delivery system, and the professional requirements for supplying health services—and will need to be followed up by implementing legislation.

Tax and Customs Administration Reform

Weak tax compliance has been a key fiscal problem in Hungary during the 1990s. Some Hungarian studies (Árvay and Vértes, 1995) suggest that the gray economy is as large as 30 percent of economic activity, and this is both the cause and the effect of high statutory marginal tax rates. Indeed, all tax revenue as a share of reported income are well below the levels that should be generated by the official tax rates (OECD, 1997c). Part of the erosion of the tax base has come from the movement of economic activity from large easy-to-tax state firms to small businesses, whose accounts are hard to monitor, and whose income is therefore hard to tax (OECD, 1995a). But, as discussed below, this erosion is also due to disincentives implicit in the tax system. Many of the tax policy measures of the mid-1990s were designed with the objective to improve tax collection through better compliance.

In addition, there was a significant effort to improve tax administration and adapt it to the new forms of economic organization. Until 1995, manpower in the tax authority (Adó ès Pènzügyi Ellenörzèsi Hivatal (APEH)) had not yet increased, the percentage of staff working on auditing was relatively small, training was mostly on the job, and there was no structured national audit strategy. In 1996, increased financial resources were allocated to APEH, and staff was increased by 8 percent. A Large Taxpayer Unit was established in January 1996. Though its activity

---

strengthening the medical examination network, establishing rehabilitation centers, and reforming the Labor Market Fund and the social assistance programs. Once the new system is in place, the government should be able to start a recertification program for those who are currently classified as temporarily disabled—whose ranks are reputed to include many long-term unemployed (Chapter X).

[20]The Act on Capacity Reduction aims at reducing excess capacity in the hospital system, excessive and inappropriate hospitalization rates, and excessive length of stay. It defines inpatient and outpatient capacity by county and for each medical specialty until 2000, when it is hoped that the formula would provide a ratio of 80–85 hospital beds per 10,000 inhabitants.

[21]The Act on Health Insurance aims at increasing the efficiency of the health system, mainly by diverting excess demand for secondary health care services toward preventive and primary care. The main points of the act are the following. First, the act classifies health treatments into three broad categories, according to the degree of patients' participation in the cost of services: (1) treatments not covered by insurance (e.g., several types of transplants, sterilization, and acupuncture); (2) treatments provided free of charge (e.g., screening, preventive, and curative services); and (3) specific situations when the institution delivering the service is authorized to collect copayments. Second, the act specifies treatment guidelines that regulate access to services. These include the requirement of a written referral for most out/inpatient treatments and the physicians' obligation to refer patients to the lowest possible level of care. Third, the act redefines the HIF's contracting procedures with, and its supervision over, the health institutions and the physicians.

[22]For example, the reform contains little incentives for health institutions to charge copayments. Therefore, it is unlikely that these will be increased to control excess demand. The law also fails to assign the HIF a broader autonomy to contract with providers for the level and composition of services it deems necessary. Therefore, a competitive market between suppliers of health care services has yet to be established.

Box 5.4. A Chronology of Reform Measures in Health Care

Year	Reform Measures
1988	Creation of the Social Insurance Fund.
1989	Private medical practice is authorized.
1990	Switch from tax-based funding to funding through compulsory insurance.
	Ownership of health facilities transferred to local governments.
	Ministry of Social Affairs and Health renamed Ministry of Social Welfare.
	Introduction of consensus management (a three–member management team composed of a medical director, an economic director, and a nursing director) in hospitals.
1991	Establishment of National Public Health Service (responsibility for local hygiene offices) transferred from LGs to central government as part of this service.
	Approval of Act on the Self-Government of Social Insurance.
1992	Social Insurance Fund separated into a Pension Fund and a Health Insurance Fund (23.5 percent health contributions—19.5 percent for employer and 4 percent for employee).
	Parliament defines eligibility conditions for health insurance.
	Family Physician Service is created and capitation-based payment introduced.
1993	Authorization of Voluntary Mutual Health Insurance.
	Self-Governments of Social Insurance are set up with employer and employee representation.
	Outpatient care remuneration based partly on a fee-for-service scheme, and hospital care remuneration on DRG-type scheme (July 1993).
	Share of Family Physician remuneration based on capitation increased to about 80 percent of total.
1994	The Act on the Hungarian Medical Chamber establishes ethical norms and procedures for doctors; general rules of contracts between health insurance and physicians; and the right for the chambers to participate in the definition of health policy and legislation.
	Government adopts the National Health Promotion Strategy.
1995	New pharmaceutical regulations introduce a Basic List of essential drugs available at high HIF reimbursement rate. Reimbursement rates and the number of drugs on the Basic List are reduced twice in 1995.
	Some closure of hospital beds is undertaken.
1996	Employer contribution rate is reduced by 1.5 percent.
	Employer responsibility in sick pay is increased from 10 days to 15 days, and employers are to contribute one-third of sick pay expenditures of their employees.
	Reductions in reimbursement rates and changes in the drugs available in the Basic List (May).
	Adoption of Act on Hospital Capacity Reduction (July). One of its objectives is to reduce hospital beds by 10,000.
	Hospital specific weights in the DRG financing scheme are eliminated.
	Eligibility for drug card is extended.
1997	Social security base is expanded to coincide with the Personal Income Tax base. Several nonwage remunerations and incomes are included.
	Reduction of employer contribution by 3 percent; adoption of a monthly payment of Ft 1,800 for every citizen—to be paid by the employer for the employees; increase of the monthly contribution ceiling from Ft 75,000 (as set in 1992) to Ft 99,000.
	Elimination of cross-financing between the HIF and the Pension Fund.
	All public funding for Investments in the Public Health Care Sector to be allocated through the Ministry of Welfare (no investment funds will be budgeted through the LGs and the HIF).
	Reductions in reimbursement rates and changes in the drugs available in the Basic List (January).
	Adoption of Institutional Law (June) and Health Insurance Law (July) by Parliament.

was limited in its first year of implementation to about 300 taxpayers in Budapest (350 in 1997), these represent 55–60 percent of the revenue collected in the capital—and Budapest produces about 70 percent of the Hungarian tax revenue. In 1997, APEH was allowed to increase its staff by an additional 20 percent, which was allocated primarily to audit and collection functions. Also, in January 1997, a national audit plan was approved, which attempted to shift the focus of audits toward medium-sized firms.

Two other administrative measures were implemented to improve collection of tax arrears. First, in early 1996, APEH was given the power to send a notification of seizure of asset to delinquent enterprises; failing that, APEH can now actually seize both tangible and intangible assets. Second, as of the second half of 1996, enterprises entitled to receive any payment from the central budget, including subsidies, first have to clear any outstanding tax liability with APEH and the SSFs. Similar seizing powers were also bestowed upon the Customs Administration (VPOP), which also considerably increased its staff in 1997 (by 14 percent).

Considerable progress has been achieved in improving tax administration, although further progress is possible.[23] In this respect, compliance and effectiveness of tax administration would be considerably helped by a simple, transparent, and stable tax environment. In a closely related area, efforts to integrate the collection and auditing of social security contributions (managed by the HIF and the PIF, respectively) and the general tax collection may generate efficiency savings by eliminating unnecessary duplications (and excessive burden on taxpayers), and should improve the capacity of authorities to detect tax evasion.

References

Árvay, Janos, and Andras Vértes, 1995, *The Share of the Private Sector and the Hidden Economy in Hungary* (Budapest: GKI Economic Research).

Goldstein, Ellen, and others, 1996, "Trends in Health Status, Services, and Finance," World Bank Technical Paper No. 341 (Washington: World Bank).

---

[23]A tax administration modernization project, focusing on an ambitious computerization program, is supported by the World Bank.

International Monetary Fund, 1996, *Government Finance Statistics Yearbook* (Washington: International Monetary Fund).

Józan, Péter E., 1996, "Health Crisis in a Society in Transition: The Hungarian Case" (mimeographed).

Ministry for Public Welfare, 1996, *Yearbook 1995* (Budapest).

National Health Insurance Fund Administration, 1994, *Statistical Yearbook 1993* (Budapest).

———, 1995, *Statistical Yearbook 1994* (Budapest).

———, 1996, *Statistical Yearbook 1995* (Budapest).

Organization for Economic Cooperation and Development, Centre for Cooperation with the Economies in Transition, 1995a, *OECD Economic Surveys: Hungary* (Paris: OECD).

———, 1995b, *Social and Labour Market Policies in Hungary* (Paris: OECD).

———, 1997a, *Health Database* (Paris: OECD).

———, 1997b, *National Accounts: 1983–1995* (Paris: OECD).

———, 1997c, *OECD Economic Surveys: Hungary* (Paris: OECD).

———, 1997d, *OECD in Figures*, supplement to *The OECD Observer*, No. 206 (June/July).

Palacios, Robert, and Roberto Rocha, 1997, "The Hungarian Pension System in Transition" (unpublished, World Bank, July).

Ruggiero, Edgardo, 1997, "Health Care Reform in Hungary," in *Hungary—Selected Issues*, IMF Staff Country Report No. 97/218 (Washington: International Monetary Fund).

Schiavo-Campo, Salvatore, Giulio de Tommaso, and Amitabha Mukherjee, 1997, "An International Statistical Survey of Government Employment and Wages," Policy Research Working Paper No. 1806 (Washington: World Bank).

United States, Social Security Administration, 1997, *Social Security Programs Throughout the World—1997* (Washington: Social Security Administration).

World Bank, 1995, "Hungary: Structural Reforms for Sustainable Growth," World Bank Country Study (Washington: World Bank).

VI Hungary's Growth Performance: Has It Lived Up to Its Potential?

Rachel van Elkan

Since 1990, as part of its transition from central planning to a market economy, Hungary implemented a comprehensive liberalization of its economic system. This liberalization was achieved by correcting relative prices through subsidy cuts, reducing trade distortions, freeing most food prices, hardening enterprise budget constraints, approving new bankruptcy and banking laws, and privatizing state enterprises. As elsewhere in the region, these reforms were accompanied in the early 1990s by a sharp drop in output and a surge in inflation. Although the transition toward a market economy is ongoing, the decline in output has been halted, and a recovery has begun. This chapter describes the main influences on the evolution of output in Hungary since 1990, and examines Hungary's future growth prospects with specific focus on the role that structural and macroeconomic policies can play in enhancing those prospects.

Growth During 1990–96

Following more than two decades of gradual reform, Hungary stepped up the pace of transition in 1990. Output began to decline that year, before falling sharply in 1991. The pace of decline moderated in 1992 and 1993—the year when output reached its lowest level. Between 1989 and 1993, GDP declined by a cumulative 18½ percent. Consistent with typical cyclical behavior during downturns, the bulk of this decline was due to a sharp drop in fixed investment (Figure 6.1). In 1993, the output decline reflected a marked deterioration in the external accounts as exports collapsed while import growth remained robust.

Thereafter, positive—though modest—output growth was restored, initially on the strength of investment and, following the implementation of the 1995 austerity program, on the contribution of the external sector, which more than offset a steep decline in private consumption. Activity subsequently accelerated sharply: GDP growth in 1997 is estimated at 4 percent, fueled by a combination of strong investment and continued expansion in the external sector.

This output growth pattern can be contrasted with those in other countries in the region. Annual GDP indices for Hungary, Poland, the Czech Republic, the Slovak Republic, and Slovenia in "stabilization time" (i.e., with the year in which stabilization was initiated in each country denoted as 0) are depicted in Figure 6.2. For Hungary, year 0 is 1990, when broad-based price liberalization (including the freeing of food prices and adjustments in energy prices) took place, financial policies were significantly tightened, and decisive structural reform efforts began.[1] The figure reveals that, in each of the advanced transition countries, output declined steeply in the first and second year following the initiation of reform, but the process of recovery three years out was well established for most of the countries in the chart. By contrast, Hungary endured four consecutive years of negative output growth during the transition. Moreover, the pace of recovery was also slower in Hungary. Specifically, by 1996, GDP had increased between 12 percent and 24 percent from its minimum level for the other countries in the chart, while in Hungary, output had recovered by only 6 percent.[2] To sum up, Hungary's depression since 1990 was longer and its subsequent recovery flatter than in other advanced transition economies.

Two factors may explain this performance: The postponement of macroeconomic stabilization to the mid-1990s and the slowing of structural reform during 1993 to mid-1995. The postponement of macro-

---

[1]Measured by the annual change in their index of liberalization, de Melo and others (1996) find that 1990 was indeed the year of most intense reform in Hungary. For the other economies, time 0 was as follows: Poland (1990); Czech Republic (1991); the Slovak Republic (1991); and Slovenia (1990).

[2]Despite the less severe nature of Hungary's recession, by 1996, its cumulative output loss was only slightly less than the average of the other advanced transition countries.

Figure 6.1. Contributions to Growth
(In percent)

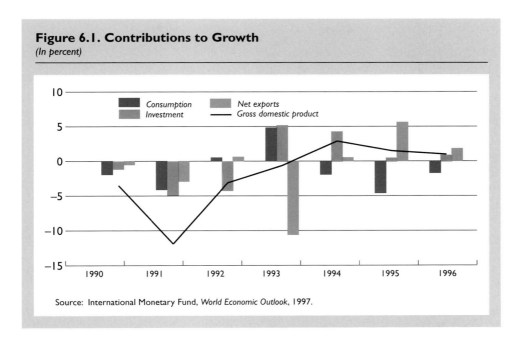

Source: International Monetary Fund, *World Economic Outlook*, 1997.

Figure 6.2. Real Output in Advanced Transition Countries
(Index; Year −1 = 100)

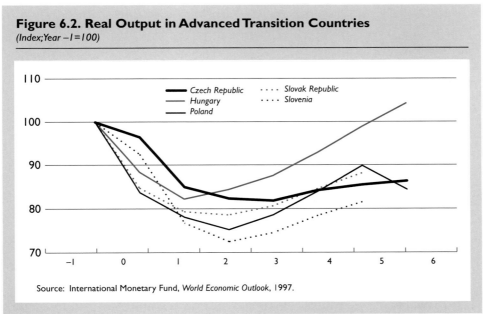

Source: International Monetary Fund, *World Economic Outlook*, 1997.

economic stabilization is apparent from a few indicators. As shown in Figure 6.3, Hungary's progress in reducing *inflation* has been relatively modest compared with other countries.[3] Hungary's current account deficit stood above 9 percent of GDP in 1993–94, compared to a surplus of 1 percent of GDP in 1990–92. Likewise, the deficit of the consolidated government stood above 7 percent of GDP in 1992–94, compared to a surplus of 1 percent of GDP in 1990 and a deficit of 3¼ percent of GDP in 1991.

To what extent did the delay in macroeconomic stabilization hamper growth performance? A tentative answer to this question may be found in the empirical literature linking growth to inflation and fiscal performance. A number of empirical studies conclude that growth is adversely affected by infla-

---

[3]Of course, Hungary was spared high inflation at the outset of reform as a result of significant progress made with price liberalization over the previous two decades.

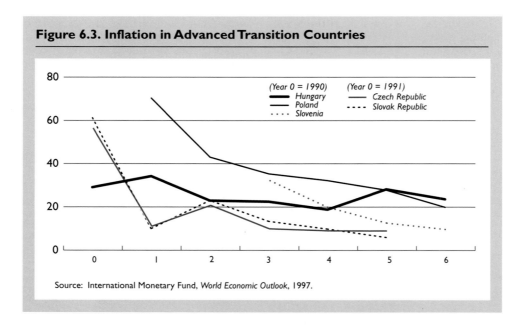

Figure 6.3. Inflation in Advanced Transition Countries

Source: International Monetary Fund, *World Economic Outlook*, 1997.

tion. Bruno and Easterly (1995) find that this negative relationship is apparent when inflation exceeds 40 percent. However, Sarel (1996) argues that growth is adversely affected by inflation rates as low as the high single digits, with a doubling of inflation from such levels lowering growth by almost 2 percentage points. Evidence presented in Box 6.1, based on a panel data set covering 25 eastern European countries, the Baltic countries, and the Commonwealth of Independent States, also suggests that both inflation and the size of government are statistically and economically significant determinants of growth performance. This evidence, in conjunction with the studies mentioned above, would suggest that Hungary's failure to achieve a sizable and sustained reduction in inflation since 1990 significantly impeded its growth performance. If one takes the average inflation rate of the advanced central and eastern European countries in 1996 and Sarel's estimates (which are based on a much broader sample than those in Box 6.1) as a base case, slow progress with inflation stabilization could have reduced Hungary's growth rate by nearly 2 percentage points.[4]

As to the effect of fiscal imbalances on growth, according to Fischer and others (1996b), transition countries that imposed more restrictive financial policies, in the form of a pegged exchange rate and a tight fiscal stance, grew faster during 1992–95. Using their estimates, the relative deterioration in Hungary's fiscal position could explain about ¾ percentage point of the growth shortfall relative to the other advanced transition countries in 1996.

In addition to the slow progress on the macroeconomic front, Hungary's growth performance may also have been affected by a slowing of structural reform from 1993 to mid-1995. By 1993, Hungary had already made significant progress in establishing a market-based economy, and was assessed by the European Bank for Reconstruction and Development (EBRD) to be among the most advanced of the transition countries in this area.[5] Among the notable achievements were that more than 90 percent of prices, weighted by their share in the consumption basket, had been freed of administrative controls; licensing and quota restrictions on trade had been virtually eliminated; small-scale privatization was almost complete; and the private sector already accounted for 50 percent of the economy. However, Hungary's reform process slowed markedly from 1993 to mid-1995, when little headway was made in ensuring the long-term viability of the social security system, restructuring the financial system, or privatization. Moreover, despite efforts at fiscal retrenchment, the size of the public sector did not decline between 1990 and 1995, with the share of consolidated government expenditure remaining at about 50 per-

---

[4]This estimate is calculated as the product of Sarel's coefficient on the logarithm of inflation (−2.48) and the difference in the logarithm of inflation in Hungary in 1996 (24 percent) and the logarithm of average inflation in 1996 in Poland, the Czech Republic, the Slovak Republic, and Slovenia (11 percent). The estimated effect of inflation on growth presented in Box 6.1, which is based on a sample of transition economies, is similar to that found by Sarel.

[5]De Melo and others (1996) confirm Hungary's ranking as among the top reformers in 1993.

cent of GDP in 1995.[6] A consequence of the still-large size of the government sector is the high level of distortionary taxes required to finance it. In particular, the tax wedge on labor income created by contributions to social security remains among the highest in the world, with negative implications for labor market participation and output growth.

The importance of maintaining the momentum of structural reform is borne out by several studies. Sachs (1996) finds that, for a group of 25 countries from eastern Europe, the Baltic countries, and the Commonwealth of Independent States, reform (measured in terms of broad-based indices of liberalization) is positively correlated with GDP growth during 1989–95 and, therefore, that greater progress in the structural area leads to a smaller cumulative output loss and/or a faster recovery in activity.[7] In addition, de Melo and others (1996) find that more than one-half the variation in growth across transition countries is related to differences in economic liberalization, with the latter's importance depending on both the *duration* as well as the *intensity* of reform. Based on the index and econometric results presented in de Melo and others (1996), Hungary's annual growth rate would have been ¼ percentage point higher had it achieved the same degree of liberalization as the Czech Republic in 1993 and in 1994.[8]

Third, Hungary's growth performance may also be related to specific elements in the design of its reform program. A case in point relates to the establishment of the Bankruptcy Law in January 1992, which, by automatically activating bankruptcy or liquidation procedures in cases where obligations were overdue by as little as 90 days,[9] forced into bankruptcy a number of economically viable firms affected solely by temporary liquidity problems.[10] Moreover, for those firms impacted by the law, bankruptcy proceedings were excessively protracted, with resolutions requiring two years on aver-age. About one-third of Hungary's industrial enterprises are estimated to have been affected by the law in 1992–93, with particularly adverse effects on output in the export sector. This is not to say, however, that Hungary's output performance would have been stronger had the law not been in place. On the contrary, the law was a key instrument in reforming the supply-side of the economy. Had some elements of the law been designed more carefully, the resulting output loss would have been more contained.

Growth in the Medium Term

This section employs an aggregate production function approach to assess the implications for Hungary's medium-term growth rate—over the next four years—of recent investments in physical and human capital and improvements in productive efficiency, given initial factor endowments and progress to date with structural reform. It argues that, while slow progress with stabilization and a loss of momentum in structural reform may have held down growth thus far, success in attracting foreign direct investment, together with human capital improvements, augur rather well for Hungary's future growth prospects, as long as policy shortcomings, such as the still high inflation rate, are rectified.

Physical Capital

As in other transition economies, Hungary's stock of physical capital at the beginning of transition was built up from a series of investments guided by motives other than profit maximization. Since these investments were largely irreversible, the stock of "effective" capital under market conditions was less than the initial stock of capital. An estimate of the effective size of the capital stock—and hence of the degree of inefficiency of past investment—can be made by determining the amount of capital required to generate Hungary's current level of output under market conditions, controlling for other factors including human capital and labor endowments.[11] Assuming that misallocated investments cannot be diverted to productive uses, Borensztein and Montiel (1991) find that three-fourths of Hungary's investment under central planning (equal, on average, to 29 percent of GDP in 1960–85) was unproductive.

The initial size of Hungary's capital stock affects its future growth prospects via the productivity of investment, with the low level of Hungary's effective

---

[6]Total government spending in 1995 remained unchanged from its 1990-GDP share because subsidy reductions were offset by increases in spending on social security and debt servicing.

[7]This is consistent with Hernandez-Cata (1997) who finds that, although the *initial* contraction of aggregate output is much steeper for a strong reformer than for a slow reformer, the subsequent recovery occurs earlier and is more rapid. On balance, he finds that the cumulative loss is lower for the strong reformer.

[8]According to indices of liberalization from de Melo and others (1996), the Czech Republic was the most advanced reformer in 1993–94, with a weighted index of 90 in each year, whereas Hungary, Poland, the Slovak Republic, and Slovenia had a weighted average index of 0.84, 0.84, 0.83, and 0.82, respectively.

[9]The automatic 90-day trigger was repealed at the end of 1992.

[10]In addition, during this period, many large state-owned enterprises were able to evade the law either because of their close links to state banks, which continued to extend credit, or through special debt-resolution channels, which entailed a large element of debt forgiveness.

---

[11]This methodology attributes all the inefficiency to capital investment and assumes that all existing capital is fully employed. Therefore, the resulting estimate may overstate the degree of wasteful investment.

Box 6.1. Growth Determinants for Transition Countries: Panel Estimates

An extensive body of theoretical and empirical literature exists on the sources of growth in developing and industrial economies. While this literature may also be relevant to countries undergoing the transition from planning to a market economy, other factors may also come into play during this process. Enterprise restructuring, price liberalization, and private sector expansion, while not unique to transition, occur at a more accelerated pace in transition countries than in other economies, with potentially important implications for economic activity.

This box presents econometric estimates of the effects of various macroeconomic and structural variables on growth using a pooled cross-section-time series data set for 10 eastern European countries and 15 countries of the Baltic countries and the Commonwealth of Independent States during 1993–96. Data availability prior to 1993 is scant for a number of countries, which dictated the relatively small number of observations per country.

The class of models used in the empirical estimations allows for the inclusion of a time-variant country-specific factor, in addition to time-varying variables that are common across countries, and is of the form:

$$g_{i,t} = \mu_i + \beta' x_{i,t} + \varepsilon_{i,t} \qquad (1)$$

where $g_{i,t}$ is the annual GDP growth rate for country i in year t, μ_i is the country-specific term, $x_{i,t}$ is the vector of explanatory variables, and $\varepsilon_{i,t}$ is a mean-zero disturbance term possibly with a time and/or group dependent variance. The country-specific term is a composite of time-invariant idiosyncratic factors affecting a country's growth rate.

The right-hand side variables to be considered below consist of policy variables, macroeconomic variables, and structural variables. The set of *policy variables* consists of the government balance as a share of GDP and year-average consumer price inflation. The *macroeconomic variables* include foreign direct investment, total and private investment, domestic credit, and the volume of trade, all as a share of GDP. The list of *structural variables* includes the share of the private sector in GDP and the ratio of government expenditure to GDP, as well as measures of progress with structural reform put together by the EBRD. These include indices of price liberalization, reform of the foreign exchange and trading systems, and enterprise restructuring.

Consistent with the findings elsewhere in the literature (as discussed earlier in this chapter), the results presented below confirm the importance for growth of: (1) a stable macroeconomic environment; and (2) progress with structural reform. The results of the preferred specification are given in equation (2) below, where t-statistics (in parentheses) are based on (White) heteroskedastic-consistent standard errors:

$$g_{i,t} = \mu_i - 0.160 govexp + 10.3 plib + 0.943 avfdi$$
$$\qquad\quad (-2.36)^* \qquad (5.48)^{**} \qquad (4.09)^{**}$$

$$- 4.10 \log(infl^L) - 3.07 \log((infl^M)$$
$$\quad (-2.44)^{**} \qquad (-3.13)^{**}$$

$$- 2.48 \log(infl^H) \qquad\qquad (2)$$
$$\quad (-3.98)^{**}$$

Adjusted R^2 = 0.748
F[30, 44] = 8.31; P-value = 0.000

---

capital stock implying a relatively high marginal product. This suggests, paradoxically, that the prospects for growth from new investment are more favorable than if efficiency under planning had been greater, and that a relatively modest investment rate could sustain relatively high rates of growth. Indeed, assuming an investment rate of 22 percent of GDP—well below the average for 1960–85 and below the current rate of 25 percent of GDP—Borensztein and Montiel's cross-country growth regressions suggest that Hungary could achieve growth rates of 5–6 percent in the future (assuming that human capital and population growth rates are the same as in 1960–85), similar to rates achieved at present by the other advanced transition economies. While such regressions are suggestive, it is nevertheless worth examining whether other approaches give similar results.

Foreign direct investment is frequently argued to be a good predictor of an economy's future growth performance, especially given FDI's role as a vehicle for the international transfer of new technologies and management practices, and the empirical evidence on the complementarities between FDI and human capital and between FDI and domestic investment (Borensztein and others, 1995).[12] Hungary has indeed been a leader in the region in attracting a large volume of FDI, with cumulative FDI during 1991–96 of $12.4 billion, almost three times as much as the next largest recipient (Russia).[13, 14] The

---

[12]Borensztein and others (1995) do not distinguish between privatization-related and other FDI.

[13]Hungary's position in attracting regional FDI flows reflects, inter alia, its relatively advanced stage of implementation of market reforms and price stabilization; its geographic proximity to major trading partners; the quality of its labor force; the size and income of its domestic market; and tax incentives to foreign investors. The importance of reform for attracting FDI is supported by a recent EBRD survey of investors (EBRD, 1995), which finds

where *govexp* is the share of primary government expenditure in GDP; *plib* is the EBRD's index of cumulative price liberalization; *avfdi* is the average of current and lagged FDI as a share of GDP; log(*infl*) is the natural log of the average of current and lagged inflation, with the superscripts *H, M, L* indicating, respectively, average inflation in excess of 40 percent, between 8 percent and 40 percent, and below 8 percent; and ** (*) indicates significance at the 1 (5) percent level.

Consistent with our theoretical priors, the results imply that an increase in both inflation and the size of government lowers growth, while an increase in FDI and progress with price liberalization both raise growth. Specifically, a 1 percentage point increase in the share of FDI in GDP raises growth by almost 1 percentage point, similar to the results of Borensztein and others (who found a coefficient of 0.8 based on a sample of nontransition countries). With respect to the cumulative price liberalization index, *plib*, which is an ordinal variable, only the *sign* of the coefficient rather than its magnitude, is of relevance. The coefficient on *plib* is positive and highly significant. Also, inflation is found to have a negative effect on growth. Moreover, the effect of inflation on growth is found to vary with the level of inflation: a doubling of inflation from a high level (say from 50 percent to 100 percent) lowers annual growth by 1.7 percent, while doubling inflation from (say) 15 percent to 30 percent reduces growth by 2.1 percent, and increasing inflation from (say) 3 percent to 6 percent lowers growth by 2.8 percent. However, caution must be used when interpreting this result since the decreasing effect of inflation on growth may reflect the large movements in inflation over the current sample, which are due to price liberalization. As a result, the coefficient on log(*infl^H*) may be picking up some of the positive growth effects associated with price liberalization, which may be imperfectly measured in the *plib* variable used in the above specification.[1] Finally, a 1 percentage point reduction in the share of government in the economy raises growth by more than 0.15 percentage point. Interestingly, the government balance was found to have no independent impact on growth, suggesting that the effects of the deficit operate through the other terms in the regression (inflation and government expenditure).

The likelihood ratio test and the F-test supports strongly the choice of a fixed-effects model over the alternative model without country dummies.[2] The country-specific parameters capture the possible effects on growth of time-independent variables, including the level of income at the beginning of transition, the cumulative decline in output, the degree of corruption, as well as specific features in the design of a country's transition process. Each of the country-specific coefficients (not reported above) is significant at the 5 percent level.

---

[1]It is noteworthy that, in an alternative specification of the model, the first difference of *plib* was found to have a highly significant negative impact on growth; in that specification, moreover, the magnitude of the coefficients on log(*infl^H*) and log(*infl^M*) were reduced, and the coefficient on log(*infl^L*) was no longer significant.

[2]The probability value is less than 1 in 100,000.

---

magnitude of FDI is even more apparent when scaled against the size of the economy, with the ratio of FDI to GDP averaging 5 percent during 1991–96, compared with an average of less than 1¼ percent in the other economies of the region.[15]

Cross-country evidence suggests an economically and statistically significant relationship between the FDI/GDP ratio and growth performance, with Borensztein and others (1995) finding that a 1 percentage point increase in the former raises growth by 0.85 percentage point.[16] In addition, empirical estimates presented in Box 6.1 would suggest a slightly larger coefficient (about unity); that is, a 1 percentage point increase in the FDI ratio raises growth by about 1 percentage point. If one assumes (conservatively) that the ratio of FDI to GDP in Hungary stabilizes at 3 percent of GDP during 1997–99 as the privatization process winds down, Hungary's average FDI ratio during the 1990s would amount to about 4 percent of GDP. Using either Borensztein's regression results or those in Box 6.1, one would

---

that countries that are comparatively advanced with reform and stabilization have attracted a relatively large share of regional FDI. Selowsky and Martin (1996) draw similar conclusions about the relationship between reform and FDI, based on the de Melo and others (1996) index of liberalization.

[14]The *quality* of Hungary's FDI, as measured by the per capita income level of the source country, was also relatively high, with Germany, the United States, and Austria contributing about 60 percent of total FDI during 1993–94.

[15]Albania, Belarus, Croatia, Czech Republic, Estonia, Latvia, Lithuania, Macedonia, FYR, Moldova, Poland, Romania, Russia, the Slovak Republic, Slovenia, and Ukraine.

[16]Estimates from Borensztein and others (1995) are based on time-averaged data over 10-year blocks. Given the lags that are likely to be present, it is sensible to assume that Hungary's future prospects will be influenced not only by future FDI but also by the relatively high rates of FDI in the past. This is the underlying assumption in the exercise below.

conclude that Hungary's medium-term growth rate is likely to be boosted by about 3 percentage points (with respect to other countries) on account of the increase in FDI alone.

Labor

The demographic profile of Hungary's population suggests that the size of the labor force will increase only marginally (0.3 percent a year) during 1997–2000. However, the effective labor supply will be boosted during this period by improvements in educational attainment. As shown in Table 6.1 below, secondary school enrollment increased markedly between 1970 and 1992, while enrollment in tertiary education also rose. The illiteracy rate also declined (albeit from a low level). Increased participation in formal education will serve to improve Hungary's growth potential by raising the average skill level of workers, since the human capital of workers entering the labor force will exceed that of those they replace through retirement.

Based on the regression results of Levine and Renelt (1992), the increase in the labor force and in secondary school enrollment from its 1980 rate should raise Hungary's medium-term potential growth rate by about ¼ percentage point. This figure probably underestimates the effect of improved education on growth in the most recent period. For example, the number of students in secondary and tertiary schools increased by 8 percent and 54 percent, respectively, during 1993–95.

Factor Productivity

A major objective of reforms undertaken during the transition is to improve total factor productivity (TFP). Structural reform can affect TFP through two channels. First, existing resources may be reallocated to more productive uses. Policies that further this objective are those that create incentives for more efficient resource allocation (e.g., subsidy reductions, smaller government); facilitate resource mobility (e.g., greater efficiency in financial intermediation); and enhance competition in the domestic economy (e.g., elimination of trade barriers, and establishment of the commercial and legal institutions of a market economy). Second, TFP can be boosted by the upgrading of technologies. Greater openness to trade and investment provides a conduit for the international transfer of advanced production techniques and technical knowledge, thereby enabling transition countries to close the technology gap with industrial countries.

Evidence from developing countries suggests that improvements in TFP have been an important factor in sustaining economic growth. Between 1971 and 1993, increases in TFP accounted for nearly one-half (1½ percentage points) of per capita growth among developing countries. Among successfully adjusting developing countries that have sustained reform, TFP's contribution to per capita growth increased to 2½ percentage points (International Monetary Fund, 1993). Individual country studies confirm the importance of reform for growth in total factor productivity. For example, in the case of Chile, Lefort and Solimano (1994) find that the contribution of TFP to output growth increased strongly in the period following the implementation of structural reforms, with the rate of growth of TFP rising from about ½ percent a year before reform to 1¼ percent thereafter.[17] In the case of Korea, Lee (1996) finds that distortionary tax/tariff incentives reduce TFP growth. Fischer (1993) finds that tariff protection weighted by the volume of trade reduces the efficiency of resource allocation.

During the transition, Hungary undertook a substantial liberalization of its trading environment, reducing average tariffs and import surcharges rapidly during 1996 and 1997 (Chapter IX). Partly in response, the degree of openness (measured by the trade ratio) has increased from 38 percent of GDP in 1990 to 70 percent of GDP in 1996. Moreover, the orientation of trade has also shifted, with 65 percent of trade now taking place with European Union countries. Based on the econometric results of Fischer (1993), greater openness and reduced protection is likely to boost future TFP growth by ¼ percentage point.

Table 6.1. Enrollment and Illiteracy Rates

	1970	1980	1992
Enrollment (percent of age group enrolled)			
Secondary school	63	70	81
Tertiary	12.9	—	15.3
(Percentage of population)[1]	0.8	0.9	1.8[2]
Illiteracy rate (percentage of population age 15 and above)	2	1	—

Source: IBRD, *World Development Indicators* (Washington: World Bank).
[1]*Statistical Yearbook of Hungary*, 1995.
[2]Figure for 1995.

---

[17]Lefort and Solimano (1994) find that the most important factors in explaining the increase in TFP growth were greater external openness (measured by reductions in import protection) and the increase in financial deepening (proxied by the real level of interest-bearing deposits in the banking system).

Removing Obstacles to Growth

Output in Hungary expanded by a modest 1 percent in 1996, largely—as argued in the previous section on growth during 1990–96—owing to slow progress with macroeconomic stabilization. Nevertheless, as discussed above, several factors suggest that Hungary is now poised to see its growth rate pick up significantly, especially because of its superior performance in attracting FDI. This said, however, future prospects will continue to be circumscribed if progress is not made in durably reducing inflation toward single-digit levels.

To make concrete the benefits to medium-term growth prospects from lower inflation, the empirical results from the previous section may be brought to bear. In their medium-term macroeconomic forecast, authorities target a gradual decline in inflation to 8 percent by 2000. Based on empirical estimates reported above and this target, the planned disinflation could raise potential growth by 1½ percentage points.[18] The analysis in the previous three subsections suggested, meanwhile, that factor accumulation (FDI, effective labor) and improvements in TFP flowing from greater openness could boost Hungary's growth rate by 3 percentage points. Therefore, decisive improvements on the stabilization front in line with authorities' targets would be consistent with a medium-term sustainable growth rate of about 6 percent.

References

Blanchard, Olivier, 1996, "Theoretical Aspects of Transition," *American Economic Review*, Vol. 86, No. 2, pp. 117–22.

Borensztein, Eduardo, Jose De Gregorio, and Jong-Wha Lee, 1995, "How Does Foreign Direct Investment Affect Economic Growth?" NBER Working Paper 5057 (Cambridge, Massachusetts: National Bureau of Economic Research).

Borensztein, Eduardo, and Peter Montiel, 1991, "Savings, Investment, and Growth in Eastern Europe," IMF Working Paper No. 91/61 (Washington: International Monetary Fund).

Bruno, Michael, and William Easterly, 1995, "Inflation Crises and Long-Run Growth," NBER Working Paper 5209 (Cambridge, Massachusetts: National Bureau of Economic Research).

de Melo, Martha, Cevdet Denizer, and Alan Gelb, 1996, "Patterns of Transition from Plan to Market," *World Bank Economic Review*, Vol. 10, No. 3, pp. 379–424.

European Bank for Reconstruction and Development, 1995, "Transition Report" (London: EBRD).

———, 1996, "Transition Report" (London: EBRD).

Fischer, Stanley, 1993, "Macroeconomic Factors in Growth," *Journal of Monetary Economics*, Vol. 32, pp. 485–512.

Fischer, Stanley, Ratna Sahay, and Carlos Végh, 1996a, "Stabilization and Growth in Transition Economies: The Early Experience," Journal of Economic Perspectives, Vol. 10 (Spring), pp. 45–66.

———, 1996b, "From Transition to Market: Evidence and Growth Prospects" (mimeo, International Monetary Fund).

Hernandez-Cata, Ernesto, 1997, "Liberalization and the Behavior of Output During the Transition from Plan to Market," IMF Working Paper No. 97/53 (Washington: International Monetary Fund).

International Monetary Fund, 1993, *World Economic Outlook* (Washington: International Monetary Fund, October).

Lee, Jong-Wha, 1996, "Government Interventions and Productivity Growth," *Journal of Economic Growth*, Vol. 1, No. 3 (September), pp. 391–414.

Lefort, Fernando, and Andres Solimano, 1994, "Economic Growth After Market-Based Reform in Latin America: The Cases of Chile and Mexico" (unpublished, World Bank).

Levine, Ross, and David Renelt, 1992, "A Sensitivity Analysis of Cross-Country Growth Regressions," *American Economic Review*, Vol. 82, No. 4, pp. 942–63.

Sachs, Jeffrey, 1996, "The Transition at Mid-Decade," *American Economic Review*, Vol. 86, No. 2, pp. 128–33.

Sarel, Michael, 1996, "Nonlinear Effects of Inflation on Economic Growth," *Staff Papers*, International Monetary Fund, Vol. 43 (March), pp. 199–215.

---

[18]Calculated on the basis of the average inflation rate during 1997–2000.

VII What Determines Inflation in Hungary? A Cross-Country Perspective

Reza Moghadam

The rise in inflation from single to double digits coincided with the onset of Hungary's transition to a market economy in the late 1980s. Unlike most other transition countries in central and eastern Europe, Hungary had introduced a series of price reforms since the late 1960s;[1] therefore, economic liberalization in the late 1980s and early 1990s did not lead to the explosion in prices seen elsewhere (Figure 7.1). Despite this favorable position, inflation in Hungary has been very sticky. Over the last seven years, it has essentially fluctuated in the 20–30 percent range.

The problems associated with persistent inflation in Hungary have been well articulated, most recently by Surányi and Vincze (1998) and Medgyessy (1998). For example, one-fourth of the Hungarian population are pensioners whose income has been only partially indexed. Low inflation is also often seen as a precondition for long-term investment and, therefore, sustainable growth. The goal of low inflation is widely accepted by the policymakers in Hungary. The Hungarian government has declared its intention to join the European Union, and there is political consensus on this issue. Achieving an inflation level close to the western European average is an important Maastricht criterion, and although this is not a condition for EU membership, it would signal the country's readiness to integrate with the European Union and eventually cope with monetary union. With the sharp reduction in the external current account deficit achieved over the past three years, the focus of economic policy will be shifting toward reducing inflation in the next few years. In this respect, it is instructive to review the experience of inflation in Hungary since the early 1990s, and attempt to identify its key determinants.

Hungary's Inflation Experience

Inflation peaked in Hungary in 1991. After the near doubling of price of household electricity and gas, the liberalization of retail prices of petroleum and diesel fuels in 1991, as well as a devaluation of 15 percent in January 1991, inflation rose to almost 40 percent in mid-1991. Then, the dissolution of CMEA and the associated economic restructuring and collapse in trade led to a decline of about 15 percent in real GDP during 1990–91. This contributed to a rapid fall in inflation to about 20 percent by mid-1992 (Figure 7.2, top panel).

During 1992–94, inflation fluctuated at about 20 percent. The economic policy stance loosened gradually during this period, at least partly reflecting the concerns of policymakers regarding the deep recession and increasing unemployment (see below). The pickup in inflation in 1995 coincided with the resumption of the pace of macroeconomic adjustment. In particular, energy prices were raised sharply (Figure 7.2, central panel), the effective VAT rate was increased, the forint was devalued, and a temporary import surcharge of 8 percent was introduced. Following the introduction of the March 1995 austerity package, financial policies were tightened considerably (see below). Inflation peaked at just over 30 percent in mid-1995 before gradually declining throughout 1996 and 1997, despite further increases in administered prices.[2] By December 1997, the 12-month inflation rate had declined to 18.4 percent.

The cumulative increase in CPI has been sharper than that of PPI since 1990 (Figure 7.2, lower panel), reflecting the rise in administered prices and VAT, and the increase in the relative price of services (which were typically underpriced in centrally planned economies (van Elkan, 1996)). Therefore, a given real product wage has been associated with a

---

[1] By 1989, the price of about 80 percent of consumer products had already been freed.

[2] In particular, household prices of electricity and gas were raised by 25 percent and 18 percent, respectively, in March 1996, and again by about 25 percent in January 1997.

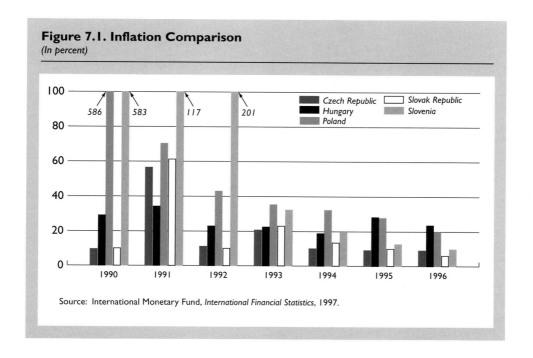

Figure 7.1. Inflation Comparison
(In percent)

Source: International Monetary Fund, *International Financial Statistics*, 1997.

comparatively lower real consumption wage over the past seven years.

What Determines Inflation?

A number of recent studies of inflation in Hungary have focused on the key macroeconomic determinants of inflation. Using time series techniques and monthly data for the period 1990:12 to 1995:12, van Elkan (1996) finds a long-run cointegrating relationship for prices that includes money, wages, and the exchange rate. This study finds that the magnitude of the effect of each of these macroeconomic factors on prices is roughly equal. Furthermore, van Elkan also discovers that changes in administered prices have had a statistically significant impact on inflation in Hungary.

Surányi and Vincze (1998) argue that the exchange rate and wage developments are the most important determinants of inflation in Hungary. They point to other empirical studies done in the National Bank of Hungary, which find that the assessment of the impact of money on inflation is complicated by the numerous structural and institutional changes since the late 1980s. Surányi and Vincze also argue that expectations have an important role in determining the inflation process in Hungary. In managing Hungary's planned economy prior to the late 1980s, policymakers had used inflation to solve demand and supply imbalances. Therefore, Surányi and Vincze argue, inflationary expectations since the

start of transition have been rekindled at any sign of macroeconomic imbalance. They also maintain that relative price changes have been an important determinant of inflation in Hungary; however, their role in explaining inflation has diminished recently. In particular, they point out that PPI and CPI have moved in tandem since early 1995 (Figure 7.3).

A Structural Perspective on Inflation

Most economists agree that inflation is a monetary phenomenon. Therefore, it would be surprising not to find a statistically significant relationship between changes in money and inflation.[3] However, such a finding is not particularly informative, as it does not necessarily reveal the reasons behind any monetary relaxation or accommodation by the authorities. Similarly, one would expect to find that movements in wages and the exchange rate are highly correlated with inflation. Again, this would tell us little about the direction of causality and how easy or difficult it is to reduce inflation in an economy with a particular wage setting structure or exchange rate regime.

To understand the phenomenon of inflation in a transition economy such as Hungary, one can ask: What are the perceived benefits of inflation, or put another way, what do authorities see as the costs aris-

---

[3]In the case of a transition country, it may be necessary, of course, to control for the structural and institutional changes that have occurred and affected money velocity and real output.

Figure 7.2. Inflation

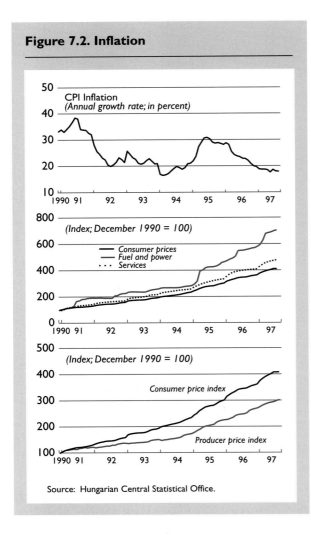

Source: Hungarian Central Statistical Office.

If the above motives or structural factors play a role, unions raise their demand above what is justified by real economic fundamentals in anticipation of the authorities' behavior.

Thus, the economy may experience an inflation bias through the wage formation mechanism. Two solutions have been found to break this vicious circle: "precommitment" and "reputation," both of which may have played a role in controlling inflation in Hungary. Precommitment could take the form of giving control of monetary policy to an independent central bank that is held accountable for price stability. Precommitment could also take the form of an exchange rate peg to a currency with a demonstrated record of low inflation. Reputation can be gained after a prolonged period of anti-inflationary stance by the authorities.

Empirical Findings

Unlike the theoretical literature, empirical evidence on the structural determinants of inflation is scant, not least because of data difficulties. Grilli and others (1991) find that central bank independence reduces inflation in industrial countries; however, Cukierman (1992) finds this relationship to be less robust when developing countries are added to the sample. Ghosh and others (1995) find that pegging the exchange rate is associated with lower inflation. With regard to transition economies, Griffiths and Pujol (1996) find support for the role of relative price adjustments in explaining inflation in Poland. Coorey and others (1996), using a panel of transition economies, find that relative prices have a statistically significant impact on inflation during the initial phase of liberalization. Fischer and others (1996) also use a panel of transition economies to find that a fixed exchange rate regime, fiscal consolidation, as well as a number of indices of economic liberalization, are associated with lower inflation.

Building on the above studies, Cottarelli and others (1998) have attempted a more comprehensive empirical study of the structural determinants of inflation, both in terms of including a larger number of structural variables and the country coverage. Their panel study uses annual data from 1993 to 1996 for 47 countries: 22 industrialized OECD countries; 10 countries from central and eastern Europe; and 15 countries from the states of the former Soviet Union. Their data set included a large number of structural variables such as information on the exchange rate regime; wage indexation; the degree of centralization in the wage bargaining system; the degree to which monetary policy is constrained by the lack of a government securities market; the degree of inde-

ing from disinflation? There is extensive academic work being done in this area. For example, Cukierman (1992) identifies four "motives" for inflation. First, unanticipated inflation could lead to an increase in output and hence employment if there are nominal rigidities in the economy. Second, higher inflation means higher seigniorage to finance the fiscal deficit. Third, a monetary expansion and subsequently a devaluation could temporarily be accompanied by a real depreciation and help to alleviate balance of payments problems. Finally, Cukierman argues that a central bank that is concerned about the health of the banking system may avoid necessary increases in interest rates (thereby contributing to rising inflation) in order to shelter financial institutions. Ball and Mankiw (1995) point to another structural factor that may be highly relevant: in the presence of "menu costs" in changing prices, asymmetric relative price shocks (such as those relating to administered price changes) could lead to higher inflation.

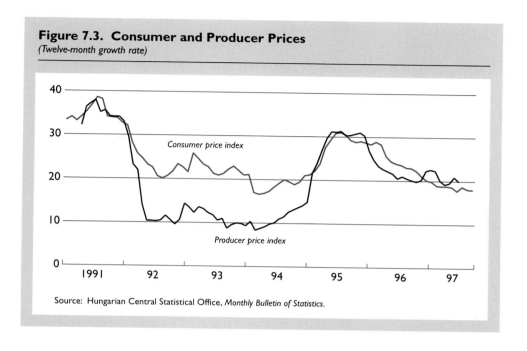

Figure 7.3. Consumer and Producer Prices
(Twelve-month growth rate)

Source: Hungarian Central Statistical Office, *Monthly Bulletin of Statistics.*

pendence of the central bank; the extent of problems in the banking sector; and relative price indicators. In addition, their model included a number of other variables suggested by the inflation motivation literature, for example, the fiscal deficit; the current account balance; and the degree of openness. Of course, not all of the above variables turned out to be significant. The key significant variables were lagged inflation, the fiscal deficit, the exchange regimes, wage indexation, central bank independence, and relative price changes. It is instructive to interpret inflation developments in Hungary in light of the behavior of these variables.

Past Inflation

Lagged inflation is significant in all specifications estimated in Cottarelli and others, with a positive sign and an elasticity of between ¼ and ⅓, indicating that high past inflation makes it more difficult to reduce current inflation. This finding is indeed not surprising in the context of Hungary, where inflation has fluctuated in a narrow band since the beginning of the transition, and the inertial character of inflation is often cited as an impediment to reducing it rapidly. This result is also consistent with the argument made by Surányi and Vincze (1998) regarding the critical role that expectations have played in keeping inflation above what is justified by economic fundamentals in Hungary.

A good example of the role of past inflation is the announcement of the 1997 inflation target (see also Chapter II). In Hungary, because of the perceived inflation inertia, the general view among policymakers and trade unions is that the inflation rate cannot be brought down by more than 4–6 percentage points a year without undue output loss. By mid-1996, the average inflation target for the year had been revised to 23½ percent, and, in line with this belief, the government announced that the target for 1997 would be set at 18 percent. During the second half of 1996, inflation dropped rapidly, in fact more rapidly than the authorities had expected, and it was already below 20 percent by the end of 1996. By then, however, the 18 percent figure for 1997 had been incorporated in expectations. Indeed, trade unions were even skeptical about achieving this target, given past experience.

Fiscal Position

Cottarelli and others find that the fiscal position is a robust explanatory variable across a number of data sets and time periods; a more expansionary fiscal stance is typically associated with higher inflation after controlling for other factors. This finding is confirmed after controlling for the endogeneity of the fiscal deficit. The fiscal deficit is not independent of inflation: if nominal interest rates on government debt are, at least to some extent, affected by inflation, interest payments and, hence, the deficit-to-GDP ratio increases with inflation. To allow for this, Cottarelli and others use the government's primary balance rather than the overall deficit as an explanatory variable.

With regard to the fiscal stance, the relatively tight fiscal policy in 1990–91 (Table 2.1, Chapter II) may have played a role in the sharp decline in inflation between mid-1991 and mid-1992. However, fiscal balances deteriorated sharply during 1992–94, reflecting the collapse in output and tax revenues and concerns of policymakers over the deep recession and the increasing unemployment: the primary balance of the consolidated government dropped by about 6 percent of GDP between 1991 and 1993. By 1994, public finances were no longer in a sustainable position (Chapter IV), fueling inflationary expectations. It is significant that nominal interest rates started rising sharply in mid-1994, possibly signaling an upward revision in inflation expectations.

The 1995–97 fiscal adjustment was initially accompanied by an increase in inflation, primarily due to the exchange rate depreciation and the adjustment in administered prices, which were necessary to redress imbalances in the real exchange rate and in domestic relative prices (see below and Chapter II). The strengthening of fiscal accounts was, however, important in containing inflationary expectations for two reasons. First, it contributed to cool consumption demand. Second, it restored the solvency of public finances, thus reducing the need for monetary seigniorage. Indeed, the improved conditions of public finances in Hungary have significantly boosted the prospects for a rapid, low-cost disinflation in the years ahead (Blanchard, 1998).

Exchange Rate Regime

Begg (1998) argues that it is difficult to assess whether transition economies that have adopted a preannounced or fixed exchange rate regime have been more successful in reducing inflation. This is because, Begg argues, many transition countries have moved to a preannounced or fixed regime only after their economic fundamentals, including inflation, have improved. However, Cottarelli and others control for a number of other economic and institutional variables and also allow for the endogeneity of the exchange rate regime by using the instrumental variables technique. They find that countries with a fixed or preannounced exchange rate regime experience a lower rate of inflation than those with a floating rate system. Thus, the precommitment to a fixed exchange rate appears to enhance anti-inflationary credibility.

Prior to 1995, the exchange rate policy in Hungary was characterized by frequent, and often ad hoc, adjustments.[4] Through these adjustments, the authori-

ties tried to strike some balance between the conflicting goals of avoiding an excessive appreciation of the real exchange rate and of containing the inflationary impact of increases in import prices. The result of this approach was poor. The lack of an announced and credible anchor for inflationary expectations did not facilitate the deceleration in wage growth that would have been necessary to achieve disinflation and external competitiveness at the same time. This approach was radically changed in March 1995. Following a devaluation of 9 percent, the March 1995 austerity package introduced a preannounced crawling peg exchange regime as an anchor for inflationary expectations. The empirical results of Cottarelli and others suggest that this step was important in the fight against inflation in Hungary.

Relative Prices

Cottarelli and others find that changes in relative prices significantly affect inflation. The pickup in inflation in Hungary in 1991 followed the liberalization of retail energy prices as well as large increases in household electricity and gas prices. The resurgence of inflation in 1995 again coincided with large increases in administrative prices, particularly energy prices (Figures 7.2, central panel, and Figure 7.4).[5]

Other Factors

Cottarelli and others find two other factors to be important in explaining inflation: (1) wage indexation leads to higher inflation; and (2) the more independent the central bank is, the lower the rate of inflation. Hungary does not have a wage indexation system, and in fact, real wages fell significantly during 1995–96 (Figure 2.7, Chapter II). However, the National Bank of Hungary has gradually gained more independence, particularly since 1995. During 1992–94, the stance of monetary policy could not have been characterized as anti-infla-

---

[4]In 1992, there were three devaluations ranging from 1.6 percent to 1.9 percent. The five devaluations in 1993 resulted in a de-

preciation of 15 percent. In 1994, there were seven devaluations for a total of 16.8 percent, including a larger-than-usual depreciation of 8 percent in August 1994, which reflected growing concerns over the size and persistence of the external current account deficit.

[5]The above evidence and the results in Cottarelli and others regarding the importance of relative price changes in inflation are somewhat at odds with the argument made by Surányi and Vincze that relative price changes may have only played an important role in the initial phase of transition in 1990–91. One possible reason for this divergent view is that Surányi and Vincze base their conclusion on statistical analysis that does not include the most recent (post-1994) period.

Figure 7.4. Administered Price Inflation
(Twelve-month growth rate)

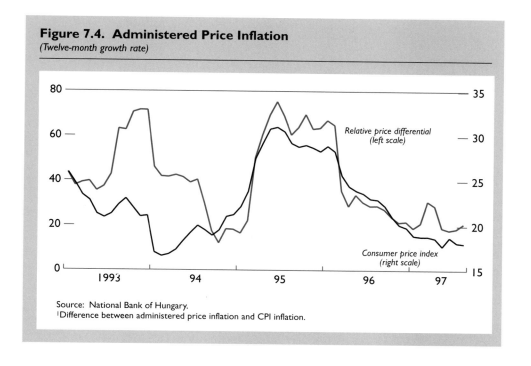

Relative price differential (left scale)

Consumer price index (right scale)

Source: National Bank of Hungary.
¹Difference between administered price inflation and CPI inflation.

tionary. Interest rates were negative in real terms between mid-1992 and the end of 1993, triggering a sharp pickup in domestic demand and thus contributing to a significant deterioration of the external current account. Although since early 1995 the conduct of monetary policy has been complicated by strong capital inflows and reverse currency substitution, the National Bank of Hungary has on the whole succeeded in keeping interest rates positive in real terms through sterilized intervention (Figure 2.3, Chapter II). In late-1996, the Central Bank Law was amended to enhance the independence of the National Bank of Hungary. This was achieved in two ways: (1) all central bank credit to the government (apart from a small temporary facility) was prohibited; and (2) through a "securitization" operation, the government swapped its large stock of non-interest-bearing liabilities to the National Bank of Hungary, which had arisen from past devaluation losses, for interest-bearing foreign exchange denominated liabilities to the central bank (Chapter IV). In fact, the operation was designed in a manner that ensured that the new stock of the National Bank of Hungary foreign exchange claims on the government was identical, in size and maturity, to the net foreign exchange position of the central bank. This strengthened the profit position and financial autonomy of the National Bank of Hungary. The increased independence of the central bank improves prospects for faster disinflation.

Conclusion

Inflation in Hungary has exhibited a large degree of inertia; this by itself has affected inflationary expectations and reduced the speed of disinflation. A number of measures that have been introduced in Hungary since early 1995 have been of critical importance in the fight against inflation. The most important of these measures are the sizable degree of fiscal adjustment between 1994 and 1997; the introduction of the crawling peg exchange regime; and the increased independence of the central bank. The rise in administered prices has also played a key role in explaining inflation. Prospects for a faster pace of disinflation are now favorable for two reasons. First, the need to increase administered prices well beyond the prevailing rate of CPI inflation is coming to an end; and second, the policies of the past three years should increase the anti-inflationary credibility or "reputation" of the authorities, thereby making further reductions in the rate of inflation less costly.

References

Ball, Lawrence, and N. Gregory Mankiw, 1995, "Relative Price Changes as Aggregate Supply Shocks," *The Quarterly Journal of Economics*, Vol. 110, Issue 1, pp. 162–93.

Begg, David, 1998, "Disinflation in Central and Eastern Europe: The Experience to Date," in *Moderate Inflation: The Experience of Transition Economies*, edited by Carlo Cottarelli and György Szapáry (Washington: International Monetary Fund and National Bank of Hungary).

Blanchard, Olivier, 1998, "The Optimal Speed of Disinflation. The Case of Hungary," in *Moderate Inflation: The Experience of Transition Economies*, edited by Carlo Cottarelli and György Szapáry (Washington: International Monetary Fund and National Bank of Hungary).

Coorey, Sharmini, Mauro Mecagni, and Erik Offerdahl, 1996, "Disinflation in Transition Economies: The Role of Relative Price Adjustment," IMF Working Paper No. 96/138 (Washington: International Monetary Fund).

Cottarelli, Carlo, Mark Griffiths, and Reza Moghadam, 1998, "The Nonmonetary Determinants of Inflation," IMF Working Paper (forthcoming; Washington: International Monetary Fund).

Cukierman, Alex, 1992, *Central Bank Strategy, Credibility, and Independence: Theory and Evidence* (Cambridge, Massachusetts: MIT Press).

Fischer, Stanley, Ratna Sahay, and Carlos Végh, 1996, "From Transition to Market: Evidence and Growth Prospects" (mimeo, International Monetary Fund).

Ghosh, Atish, Anne-Marie Gulde, Jonathan D. Ostry, and Holger C. Wolf, 1995, "Does the Nominal Exchange Rate Regime Matter?" IMF Working Paper No. 95/121 (Washington: International Monetary Fund).

Griffiths, Mark, and Thierry Pujol, 1996, "Moderate Inflation in Poland: A Real Story," IMF Working Paper No. 96/57 (Washington: International Monetary Fund).

Grilli, Vittorio, Donato Masciandaro, and Guido Tabellini, 1991, "Political and Monetary Institutions and Public Financial Policies in the Industrial Countries," *Economic Policy* (October).

Medgyessy, Peter, 1998, "Introductory Remarks," in *Moderate Inflation: The Experience of Transition Economies*, edited by Carlo Cottarelli and György Szapáry (Washington: International Monetary Fund and National Bank of Hungary).

Surányi György, and János Vincze, 1998, "Inflation in Hungary (1990–1997)," in *Moderate Inflation: The Experience of Transition Economies*, edited by Carlo Cottarelli and György Szapáry (Washington: International Monetary Fund and National Bank of Hungary).

van Elkan, Rachel, 1996, "Inflation Inertia in Hungary," in *Hungary—Selected Issues*, IMF Staff Country Report No. 96/109 (Washington: International Monetary Fund).

VIII Privatization

Rachel van Elkan

Since 1990, when Hungary's privatization program began in earnest, 45 percent of previously state-owned enterprises (SOEs) have been fully privatized and about 17 percent have been partially privatized (Table 8.1). While most of these privatizations represent small and medium-sized enterprises, Hungary has also made considerable progress in privatizing large firms in strategic sectors, including energy, banking, chemicals, and pharmaceuticals. By mid-1997, the public sector had divested itself of about 70 percent of the book value of its original holdings. Further progress has been made in the second half of 1997, with privatization receipts largely exceeding the initial projections for the year.

In designing its privatization strategy, Hungary opted primarily for a cash-based approach to improve public sector finances; moreover, it relied heavily on foreign investors to attract needed foreign exchange and to bring state-of-the-art expertise and technology to the domestic economy. Consequently, cash revenue from privatization has averaged about 3 percent of annual GDP since 1990, of which more than 80 percent was in foreign currency (Table 8.2).

This chapter discusses the evolution of Hungary's privatization process, including the early period of spontaneous privatization, the slowdown that followed, and the more recent acceleration. In addition, it looks to the future of privatization and the role of the state in the private sector-dominated economy.[1]

Early Progress

Despite an early start relative to other countries in the region, privatization in Hungary proceeded slowly at first. Adoption in 1988 of the Company Act and the Foreign Investment Act, which offered incentives for private investors and for the formation of private companies, triggered a process of "spontaneous" privatization, whereby profitable assets of state enterprises were split off and sold primarily to company insiders. To prevent this practice and to lay the basis for an orderly transformation of enterprise ownership, the Transformation Act was passed in the following year, which encouraged enterprises to establish themselves into joint-stock companies.

The government then proceeded with privatization along three tracks. First, in 1990, 20 large firms were marketed primarily to strategic foreign investors. Second, a program to privatize about 430 small and medium-sized companies was initiated in 1991. Third, about 10,000 small-scale units with less than 10 employees (mostly shops and restaurants) were also slated for privatization. The net result of this three-track approach was mixed. Of the 20 large firms, only 6 had been privatized by 1993, while another 5 were bankrupt; for the medium-sized companies, only 75 had been sold. Small-scale privatization

---

Table 8.1. Divestiture of State Enterprises
(As of June 1997)

State-owned enterprises on January 1, 1990	1,857
State-owned enterprises established since January 1, 1990	399
State-owned enterprises to be divested	2,256
Of which:	
Liquidated/dissolved	678
Fully privatized	994
Under long-term asset management	148
Enterprises remaining in state ownership	5
Transformed companies remaining in state ownership	431
Of which:	
More than 50 percent state owned	204
Less than 50 percent state owned	227
Of which:[1]	
State to retain long-term share	116
State to retain single golden share	27

Source: State Privatization Agency.
[1] According to the 1997 revision to the Privatization Law.

---

[1] The issue of privatization is also discussed in Chapter XI, with reference to state-owned banks.

Table 8.2. Revenues from Privatization[1]
(In billions of forint)

	1990	1991	1992	1993	1994	1995	1996	Jan.–June 1997	Cumulative
Total revenue	0.7	31.4	74.3	173.8	130.3	474.0	158.0	119.6	1,162.1
Cash[2]	0.6	30.3	63.0	134.9	36.8	451.6	113.9	112.5	943.6
Foreign exchange	0.5	24.6	41.0	110.7	12.9	412.1	77.5	83.8	763.1
Forint	0.1	5.7	22.0	24.2	23.9	39.5	36.4	28.7	180.5
Credit	0.0	1.0	9.1	21.7	29.3	3.9	2.4	0.3	67.7
Compensation coupons	0.0	0.0	2.3	17.3	64.2	18.5	41.6	6.8	150.7
Memorandum items:									
Average exchange rate	63.2	74.7	79.0	91.9	105.2	125.7	152.6	180.0	...
Revenues in foreign exchange (In billions of U.S. dollars)	0.0	0.3	0.5	1.2	0.1	3.3	0.5	0.5	6.4

Source: State Privatization and Asset Management Agency.
[1] Revenues accruing directly to the State Privatization and Asset Management Agency.
[2] Includes dividends and other income.

was more successful, with about three-fourths of the 10,000 units having been sold by the end of 1992.

With no new companies on offer, foreign investment dried up by mid-1993. To revive foreign exchange inflows, a 30 percent share of MATAV (Hungarian Telecom) was sold at the end of 1993 (for $875 million), which represented the first sale of a strategic Hungarian company and the largest single privatization transaction at the time in eastern Europe. Meanwhile, flagging domestic involvement in privatization led to the introduction of a preferential privatization-related credit scheme and to a system of vouchers, known as compensation coupons, which could be used to purchase shares in selected companies as restitution for the nationalization of property. Nonetheless, interest in privatization continued to wane in 1994 and in the first half of 1995 following the public reversal of several privatization deals. As a result, noncash methods were the primary form of privatization during that period. By the end of 1994, only one-third of state assets, mainly in small and medium enterprises, had been sold.

A New Direction for Privatization Since 1995

The 1995 Privatization Law

Privatization regained momentum in the second half of 1995, following the adoption of a new Privatization Law, which sought to complete the process by the end of 1997. Under the law, the range of assets to be privatized was expanded by reducing the previously mandated minimum state shareholdings in specified enterprises.[2] In addition, greater emphasis was to be accorded to cash sales of enterprises through the use of simple and transparent bidding procedures, with less recourse to nonpecuniary conditionality, including preserving employment levels in newly privatized firms.[3] While a significant discretionary element remained, privatization was to proceed along a number of clearly defined tracks, depending on the size of the company and the State's ownership stake.

The law also established a new agency, the State Privatization and Asset Management Agency (APV Rt), jointly responsible for privatization and asset management, which was formed by merging the State Property Agency and the State Asset Management Agency. At its inception, the APV Rt held a majority interest in 171 large and 259 small and medium-sized enterprises, and a minority interest in 145 large and 176 small and medium-sized enter-

---

[2] As a result, the amount of state equity that could be privatized was increased by Ft 475 billion, to about Ft 1.3 trillion (about 80 percent of the State's equity holdings in enterprises held by the State Privatization and Asset Management Agency (APV Rt) upon its founding in 1995).

[3] In the case of large companies in which the State had a majority holding, shares were to be divested through a public tendering process; in cases where the State had a minority holding, remaining shares were to be offered to current private owners, followed by the enterprise itself, before being sold by auction of public tender. For details governing the sale of small firms, see section below.

prises, with a total value of about Ft 1.6 trillion. The new agency was put under the control of the minister without portfolio responsible for privatization, a post that was created at that time to elevate the political profile of privatization.[4]

Large-Enterprise Privatization

Under the new framework, privatization accelerated, resulting in cash sales of about Ft 440 billion in the fourth quarter of 1995, of which more than 90 percent was in the form of foreign exchange. The bulk of this revenue was attributable to the sale of large strategic enterprises in the energy, financial, and infrastructure sectors, including large minority shares in six electricity-generating companies, majority stakes in five regional gas-distribution companies, an additional share of the telecommunications company, MATAV, and a majority share of Budapest Bank (all to strategic investors), as well as further divestment of the oil company (MOL) to institutional investors.[5] The privatization of the energy sector was also facilitated by new energy pricing rules, which aimed to increase energy prices to world levels by 1997, while ensuring an 8 percent return on equity in the energy sector. This policy necessitated several large step increases in gas and electricity prices between 1995 and early 1997, with subsequent increases to occur regularly to take account of exchange rate movements and changes in input costs.

Reflecting the substantial divestment in the previous year and the consequently smaller stock of assets remaining in state hands, the pace of privatization slowed somewhat in 1996. Nonetheless, a number of large enterprises in the industry, tourism, and banking sectors, as well as further segments of the energy sector, were sold during the year, netting cash revenues of about Ft 115 billion, of which about 70 percent was in foreign exchange.[6]

Despite the planned winding down of the privatization process, cash revenues from privatization are currently projected to pick up in 1997 (to about Ft 300 billion, against an initial target of Ft 180 billion) in response to a final sell-off of remaining state assets. Revenues in the first half of the year were about Ft 100 billion, reflecting primarily the success of global offerings of MOL and Richter Gideon shares.[7]

Small-Enterprise Privatization

To accelerate the sale of smaller enterprises, the 1995 Privatization Law established a separate two-step "simplified" procedure for the privatization of companies with share capital of less than Ft 800 million and fewer than 500 employees. In the first round, cash-only bids would be acceptable through public tender, with the sole condition that the bid price be at least 50 percent of the nominal book value of the shares on offer. If unsuccessful, a second round would be open to noncash bids, including the use of preferential credit, installment payments, leasing, compensation coupons, and employee buyouts. Under this simplified scheme, 25–100 percent of the shares in 140 companies (from a portfolio of 300 enterprises that qualified for the scheme) were offered for sale, netting revenues of about Ft 12 billion, mostly from Hungarian investors.

Use of Privatization Receipts

In accordance with the guidelines in the budget law, the bulk of cash revenues from privatization and dividends accruing to the APV Rt in 1995–96 was transferred to the state budget and, together with privatization receipts accruing directly to the Ministry of Finance,[8] were used to reduce public sector debt.[9] Total transfers from the APV Rt to the budget from privatization revenues earned during 1995–96 amounted to about Ft 375 billion (about 5 percent of GDP),[10] and a further Ft 150 billion from current receipts is expected to be transferred in 1997. The bulk of these transfers has been used to retire government debt owed to the National Bank of Hungary, in proportion to the structure of the debt outstanding at the end of 1995. Since most of the outstanding National Bank of Hungary credit to the government was in the form of interest-free or low-interest loans (arising primarily from devaluation-related losses), re-

---

[4]This post has since been subsumed by the Minister of Industry, Trade, and Tourism.

[5]The largest single deal involved the sale of a further 37 percent of the equity in MATAV, which raised $850 million. Sale of the five regional gas distributors, and the six electricity distributors and two generators, raised $460 million and $1.3 billion, respectively. Privatization of MOL and Budapest Bank raised $180 million and $90 million, respectively.

[6]Among the large companies sold during 1996 were the chemical companies—Borsodchem and TVK; the rubber and tire maker—Taurus; the Forum and Gallert hotels; and the Hungarian Credit Bank (MHB).

---

[7]Following this latest round of MOL privatization, the State's share was reduced by 19 percent to just below 40 percent, which netted revenues of Ft 56 billion. A 57 percent stake in Kereskedelmi es Hitelbank, the last of the remaining large state-owned commercial banks to be privatized, was sold in September 1997 for $90 million.

[8]State-owned shares in consolidated banks (MHB, K&H, Mezobank, and Takarekbank) are owned directly by the Ministry of Finance, and revenues from the sale of these assets accrue directly to the Ministry.

[9]The amount transferred by the APV Rt to the budget is equal to cash revenues less operating expenses, the direct costs of privatization, and expenditures for certain items (including enterprise restructuring) up to an amount specified in the state budget.

[10]From cumulative cash receipts of about Ft 570 billion.

Table 8.3. Composition of the State Privatization and Asset Management Agency's Cash Expenditure
(In percent of total)

	1995	1996	Jan.–June 1997	Cumulative
Direct privatization and asset management expenses	5.2	3.9	15.7	5.9
Operating expenses	1.4	1.3	1.9	1.4
Payments to local governments	1.0	7.2	17.6	6.3
Payments on outstanding guarantees	1.6	0.9	0.0	1.0
Reorganization-related cost and investment funds	7.8	10.8	8.5	9.4
Net transfer to central budget (from privatization)	67.1	64.2	0.0	56.9
Net transfer to central budget (dividends)	2.5	3.3	12.7	4.3
Other	21.6	22.2	46.4	25.2
Of which:				
Repayment of State Privatization and Asset Management Agency's debt	9.2	0.0	0.0	3.4
Repayment of enterprise debt	0.0	0.0	14.0	1.8
Retirement of government debt (E-loans)	8.3	13.9	9.3	11.2
Utilization of reserve fund for guarantees	1.6	0.8	0.0	1.0
Memorandum item:				
Total cash expenditure (in billions of forint)	223.4	298.9	78.6	600.9
(As percent of GDP)	4.0	4.5	1.0	9.5

Source: State Privatization and Asset Management Agency.

tirement of this debt substantially raised the average cost of credit from the National Bank of Hungary. Transfers to the central budget account for more than 60 percent of the APV Rt's expenditures to date (Table 8.3). Other major expenditure categories include enterprise restructuring (9½ percent of total expenses or ¾ percent of GDP), payments directly related to the privatization process (including consultants' fees), the cost of managing the APV Rt's portfolio (6 percent of total expenses), operating costs of the APV Rt (1½ percent of expenses), and cash payments to local governments (6¼ percent of total expenses) (see below). In addition, the APV Rt has set aside Ft 31 billion to cover contingent obligations (including for environmental cleanup) under already concluded privatization contracts, from which Ft 6 billion has already been drawn.

Obligations to Local Governments, Privatized Firms, and Holders of Compensation Coupons

To promote privatization and to compensate local governments and individuals for the sale or confiscation of their property, the APV Rt is legally obliged to transfer a portion of the proceeds from privatization to privatized enterprises, local governments, and individuals who suffered under previous political systems. The majority of these transfers

(about Ft 100 billion) is due to local governments under three separate legal provisions: (1) as compensation for the municipal land on which privatized enterprises are located and to cover their rights as founding owners of the privatized firms (about Ft 60 billion, of which Ft 22 billion was paid in 1996); (2) 25 percent of the shares in the electricity supply companies; and (3) 40 percent of the shares in the regional gas supply companies. The first two obligations will be settled in cash; the other will involve a transfer of assets.

Payment obligations to privatized firms are governed by the 1989 Transformation Act, which states that enterprises that transformed themselves into joint-stock companies prior to 1992 are to receive 20 percent of subsequent privatization revenues arising from their sale. More than 1,000 firms, including those that netted the largest privatization revenues, are potentially eligible for a payout, which could total more than Ft 30 billion.

The third group eligible for transfers of shares in state enterprises are holders of compensation coupons. Between 1990 and mid-1997, about Ft 150 billion of shares in state enterprises had been exchanged for coupons, and an additional Ft 80 billion have yet to be issued or redeemed.[11]

---

[11]In addition, shares and real estate were transferred to the Social Security Funds in 1996 and 1997.

Winding Down the Process Beyond Mid-1997

While the original Privatization Law envisaged the completion of the privatization process by the end of 1997,[12] the task of privatization was expanded through an amendment to the law, which was passed in July 1997. According to the modification, the State's minimum long-term holdings in a number of key enterprises are to be reduced from 50 percent and 25 percent to a single golden share.[13] As a result, the nominal book value of assets to remain in permanent state ownership fell from about Ft 350 billion to Ft 200 billion, equivalent to about 3 percent of GDP.[14] The efficiency benefits of reducing long-term state ownership in key firms in the banking, telecommunications, and energy sectors may be quite substantial; however, through its golden share, the State will retain considerable control over the broader operations of these companies.[15]

[12]In particular, it was decided that the privatization of the Hungarian Electricity Works, MVM, and the shipping company, MAHART, would be postponed until 1998.

[13]About 80 companies are affected by the amendment, of which 40 have seen the permanent government share reduced to a single golden share, while in 12 companies, long-term state ownership has been eliminated; 10 companies have seen their share rise; and 18 companies have been added to the list, mostly requiring a single golden share. Under this amendment, the number of companies in which the State is to retain a long-term share increased from 109 to 116, and the number of companies in which the State is to hold a golden share rose from 20 to 27.

[14]This further divestment is in addition to about Ft 500 billion of assets still to be privatized under the old law.

[15]The rights associated with a golden share include the power to veto changes in product lines and in the financial structure of the company, including mergers, divestments, and share conversions.

IX Trade Liberalization in Hungary

Perry Perone

As for many other aspects of the Hungarian economy, the process of trade liberalization was characterized by gradualism. Indeed, the greater openness of Hungary compared with other economies of the region was the result of a shift toward a market economy that began on the trade liberalization front in the late 1960s. While some momentum for trade reform was lost in the 1970s as a result of external economic conditions and internal political resistance, Hungary was a signatory to the General Agreement on Tariffs and Trade (GATT) in 1973, and some reforms were attempted in the decade. There were continuing attempts at introducing market mechanisms in the early 1980s, but the deteriorating economic situation made further progress difficult. Since 1989, however, as a result of the changes in the political and economic environment, Hungary has entered into several important trade agreements and has expanded its trade with market-based economies. In addition to being a charter member of the World Trade Organization (WTO) and committing to tariff bindings under the Uruguay Round, Hungary concluded an association agreement with the European Union. Along with unilateral trade liberalization measures, the commitments arising from these agreements have quickened the trade liberalization process.

Overview of the Trade Regime, 1960–97[1]

The Hungarian economy was relatively open even in the central planning period, although the patterns of trade were disproportionately weighted toward CMEA countries. Throughout the 1960s, the limits to the strategy of economic growth through extensive industrialization and centralized economic management had become increasingly obvious to the authorities. As a result, as early as 1968, the authorities launched an economic program that aimed to intro-

duce certain elements of a market economy. In the area of trade, the authorities attempted to create a link between the national economy and international markets, but the reforms were primarily limited to certain areas of economic management. The idea was that planned import quotas would be abolished so that companies requiring imports could apply for and receive, automatically, import licenses. In addition, they would be allowed to buy the requisite foreign exchange. This attempt, however, was reversed in the next few years, and the system of control and management of trade remained, to a large extent, unchanged in practice.

During the 1970s, some of the momentum for reform and liberalization that derived from experiments in the late 1960s was lost as a result of external economic conditions (primarily the increase in oil prices) and internal political pressures.[2] The system of protection developed in the 1970s relied on complex and "informal" methods of rationing rather than on tariffs or explicit quotas. The level of licensed imports was determined by the previous year's imports. To increase imports, difficult bargaining was required, such as showing what losses would be incurred in the absence of more imports (Nagy, 1994).

Some progress was made during the decade. In 1972, Hungary introduced a scheme of tariff preferences in favor of developing countries, covering products such as meat, fish, dairy, and aluminum. In 1973, Hungary acceded to the GATT on the basis of tariff concessions. Its Protocol of Accession, however, contained a number of provisions that reflected the fact that the country was not a market economy at the time. Hungary also became a signatory to the Multi-Fiber Agreement and concluded a free trade area agreement with Finland in 1974. Beginning in 1978, Hungary extended duty-free treatment to im-

---

[1]For more details on the evolution of trade policy and trade agreements entered into by Hungary, see OECD (1996) and GATT (1991).

[2]In the 1970s, the large external debt burden began to be accumulated. This was the result of a dramatic deterioration in the terms of trade related to increases in energy prices, weak export performance, and the authorities' policy choices in response to external shocks. By the end of the 1970s, Hungary's external debt stood at about $10 billion.

ports originating in the developing countries. Hungary signed all the Tokyo Round Codes, except for the Agreements on Subsidies, Government Procurement, and Civil Aircraft.

The worsening of economic conditions during the 1980s hampered the trade liberalization process. The Polish military coup in 1982 created a serious balance of payments crisis for Hungary that was a turning point (for the worse) in the import licensing system. As a result, import licenses were issued on a discretionary basis and even when licenses were granted, the foreign exchange was not always made available immediately, a problem related to the unwillingness to devalue the forint. In the face of weak export performance and energy-price related terms of trade losses, gross foreign debt increased to about $21 billion by the end of 1987.

Beginning in 1989, trade liberalization was accelerated and deepened, since it was seen as a critical element for initiating systemic changes in the context of still-emerging market structures. The initial plan had been to liberalize convertible currency imports gradually over a four-year period—between 1989 and 1992—in 20–25 percent increments. In the event, the process was completed in only three years. Imports of investment goods were liberalized in 1989, intermediate goods in 1990, and a significant proportion of consumer goods sectors were open to international competition in 1990. As of 1990, about 70 percent of production had to face import competition, and by 1991, quotas covered only 10 percent of imports. Interestingly, the reform was not linked to a drastic devaluation or to a significant increase in tariff rates. This was largely the result of the Hungarian economy being already more open than other central and eastern European countries and therefore requiring a less drastic redistribution of resources.

From January 1, 1991, the two-tier nature of Hungary's trade policy regime—in which a distinction was made between so-called convertible and nonconvertible currency trade—was replaced with a unified system. Since then, Hungary's trade with all countries (including the remaining centrally planned economies) is now also conducted in convertible currencies on the basis of world market prices and general rules, including the most-favored-nation (MFN) clause.[3]

Trade liberalization continued in the following years as a result of regional and global agreements and unilateral trade measures. Much impetus to trade reform has resulted from regional agreements, in particular, the Europe Agreement (EA) signed with

the EU in December 1991 (with the Interim Agreement regulating trade aspects having been applied since March 1992); the Free Trade Agreement with the European Free Trade Association (EFTA) countries (in force since October 1993); and the Central European Free Trade Agreement (CEFTA) concluded with the Czech Republic, Poland, and the Slovak Republic, which has been in force since March 1993 (and with Slovenia since January 1996). More recently, the authorities implemented a new tariff agreement, aligned with the Common Customs Tariff of the European Union effective January 1, 1996. The Uruguay Round Agreements consolidated the results achieved by these regional agreements by widening the geographical coverage and expanding liberalization principles to some new areas of trade relations.

As a founding member of the WTO in January 1995, Hungary started to implement its Uruguay Round commitments since this date. These include, in particular, further tariff bindings:[4] from 89 percent of tariff lines bound before the Uruguay Round (90 percent of industrial products and 25 percent of agricultural products), the number was increased to 93 percent of total tariff lines. Duty-free imports will increase from 19 percent to 21 percent of total imports. The MFN average tariff level will decrease for industrial products from 9.6 percent in 1996 to 6.9 percent by 2001, while owing to tariffication, tariffs on agricultural products will increase on average to 45 percent (from 22 percent pre-Uruguay Round).[5] Customs duties on industrial imports from the European Union and the EFTA into Hungary have been gradually lowered and will be abolished by December 31, 2000, at the latest. Under the agreement with CEFTA countries, duties for more than 80 percent of industrial products were abolished as of January 1, 1996. All trade in industrial goods (with a few exceptions) between CEFTA members will be free by January 1, 2000, and trade in agricultural goods will be liberalized substantially. Hungary had also applied, since 1973, three different kinds of foreign trade-related fees (viz., a 1 percent licensing fee, a 2 percent customs fee, and a 3 percent statistical fee). These fees have been progressively reduced, and were eliminated early in 1997.

---

[3]The most-favored-nation clause states that the contracting parties are bound to grant each other treatment as favorable as they extend to any other country regarding the application of import and export duties and other trade regulations.

[4]A tariff line is bound when the authorities commit not to raise the tariff on the particular good above the level set in the Tokyo or Uruguay Round. In many cases, the bound level is set well above the actual level of the tariff.

[5]Among industrial products, tariff reductions of more than 30 percent affect chemicals, textiles and clothing, footwear, nonelectric machinery, and metals. After the agreed reductions, the following categories will have a tariff level above the 6.9 percent average: transport equipment (16.9 percent), electric machinery, textiles and clothing, and fishery products.

Despite this progress, there were some setbacks. The most important one was the introduction in March 1995 of an 8 percent import surcharge (Chapter II), which applied to imports from all sources and covered all goods, except primary energy products, and was reimbursable in the case of imports of machinery for investment purposes and imports for re-export. The surcharge was eliminated at the end of June 1997 after having been reduced in the second half of 1996.

The overall result of the above agreements and measures was a significant reduction in the average tariff rate during the most recent period. The average tariff rate (computed as a ratio of tariff and duty revenues to imports) declined to about 5 percent in 1997, and is projected by the Ministry of Finance to fall further in 1998 (Figure 9.1).

As to import quotas, the global quota on imports of selected consumer goods (which has been in force since Hungary's accession to the GATT) amounted in 1989 to $200 million, and was raised to $750 million in both 1993 and 1994. In 1994, the global con-sumer quota included clothing, footwear, jewelry, household detergents, and fishery products. In 1995, several categories of products were withdrawn from the global quota, which implied a reduction in the quota in U.S. dollar terms. In 1996 and 1997, the product coverage stayed the same as in 1995, but the overall value of the quota was raised in 1996 to about $560 million and again in 1997 to about $640 million (Table 9.1). Further liberalization of import quotas will be completed for some products in accordance with the EU Association Agreement by the end of 1997.

Finally, all export licensing (other than for industrial products required for Hungary's international obligations) was terminated as of January 1, 1997.

Sectoral Effects of Trade Liberalization

In addition to looking at the average tariff rate, it is also useful to analyze sectoral tariff rates, taking into account trade relations across sectors. Unfortunately, reflecting data limitations, the following section focuses only on the 1990–94 period.

Effective Rate of Protection—Concept and Formula for Calculations

Effective protection is defined as the increment in value added at market prices made possible by the structure of protection as a proportion of the free trade value added. The formula can be derived as described in Cordon (1971, pp. 35–37).

Let:

P_v^{ft} = Value added per unit of j in activity j in the absence of tariffs (i.e., at the free trade effective prices),

P_v^d = Value added per unit of j, in activity j made possible by the tariff structure (i.e., the effective price after tariffs have been imposed),

g_j = Effective protection rate for activity j,

P_j = Nominal price of a unit of j in free trade,

a_{ij} = Share of i in the cost of j at free trade prices,

a_{ij}^d = Share of i in the cost of j after tariffs have been imposed,

t_j = Nominal tariff rate on j, and

t_i = Nominal tariff rate on i.

The following definitions hold:

$$P_v^{ft} = P_j(1-a_{ij}), \qquad (1)$$

Figure 9.1. Various Measures of Protection

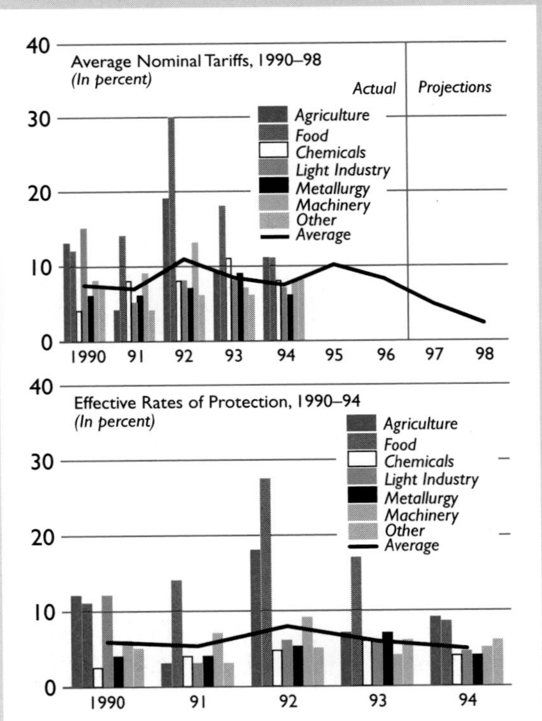

Average Nominal Tariffs, 1990–98
(In percent)

Actual | Projections

Agriculture
Food
Chemicals
Light Industry
Metallurgy
Machinery
Other
Average

1990 91 92 93 94 95 96 97 98

Effective Rates of Protection, 1990–94
(In percent)

Agriculture
Food
Chemicals
Light Industry
Metallurgy
Machinery
Other
Average

1990 91 92 93 94

Sources: National Bank of Hungary; Ministry of Finance; Ministry of Industry and Trade; and IMF staff estimates.

Table 9.1. Global Quota on Consumer Goods
(In millions of U.S. dollars, except where indicated)

	1995	1996	Jan.–June 1997	Proj. Year 1997
Household detergents	25	35	23	45
Footwear	65	70	39	77
Overwear	94	104	57	114
Secondhand clothing	27	29	16	32
Other clothing	65	71	39	78
Haberdashery products	17	17	11	23
Textile goods, carpets	43	47	26	52
Jewelry, precious metals	33	34	19	38
Fish, canned fish	23	23	17	33
Other manufactured products	126	133	73	146
Used cars and vans (in thousands of units)	53	55	29	59
New cars and vans (in thousands of units)	81	84	45	90
Total	518	563	319	638

Sources: Ministry of Industry and Trade; and IMF staff estimates.

$$P_v^d = P_j[(1+t_j)-a_{ij}(1+t_i)], \qquad (2)$$

$$g_i = \frac{P_v^d - P_v^{ft}}{P_v^{ft}}. \qquad (3)$$

Combining the first three equations gives:

$$g_i = \frac{t_j - a_{ij}t_i}{1 - a_{ij}}. \qquad (4)$$

Since the coefficients obtained from the input/output tables are those that arise in the presence of tariffs, a relationship between the so-called free-trade technical coefficient and the so-called distorted one must be made. The following expression establishes this link:

$$a_{ij}^d = a_{ij}\left(\frac{1+t_i}{1+t_j}\right). \qquad (5)$$

The formula used in this chapter can then be derived by substituting (5) into (4):

$$g_i = \frac{t_j - a_{ij}^d\left(\frac{1+t_j}{1+t_i}\right)}{1 - a_{ij}^d\left(\frac{1+t_j}{1+t_i}\right)}. \qquad (6)$$

Data and Methods

Input/output tables for 1990–93 were obtained from the National Bank of Hungary, while tariff and duty collections for 1990–94 were provided by the Ministry of Finance. It should be noted that the tariff rates used in these calculations are the implicit tariff rates, which are obtained by dividing the tariff and duty revenues by the value of imports. Thus, while implicit tariffs might show increases in some years, this could be the result of the desirable elimination of loopholes or exemptions.[6] Import data was provided by the Ministry of Industry and Trade and is based on customs data rather than balance of payments data.[7] In the case of 1994, the input/output coefficients used were from the 1993 matrix since there is no input/output table available for 1994. This implicitly assumes that the structure of production did not change between 1993 and 1994.

Calculations were performed for six broad economic sectors dictated by the availability of data: agriculture, food processing, chemicals, light industry, metallurgy, and machinery. The remaining observations were classified under a residual "other" category.

Results

Both implicit nominal and effective rates of protection by sector are presented for 1990–94 in Table 9.2. Overall, the simple average implicit nominal tariff declined by about 1 percentage point, from 9 percent to 8 percent between 1990 and 1994. Based

[6]Implicit tariff rates were employed rather than stated nominal tariffs because of data availability problems at the sectoral level regarding the latter.

[7]In Hungary, trade flow data from custom sources and from balance of payments sources differ significantly. The difference cannot be fully accounted for, but arises in part from the exclusion in the customs data of imports of goods for reexport and the subsequent exports.

Table 9.2. Nominal and Effective Rates of Protection
(In percent)

	1990	1991	1992	1993	1994
Effective rate of protection					
Agriculture	12.12	3.61	18.42	8.10	9.57
Food processing	10.56	14.16	28.68	16.90	9.44
Chemical industry	2.57	4.61	4.84	6.10	3.71
Light industry	11.78	3.66	5.95	5.78	4.69
Metallurgy	4.38	4.59	5.41	6.79	3.70
Machinery	5.92	6.84	9.46	4.44	5.20
Other	5.04	3.72	5.34	5.60	6.85
Simple average	7.48	5.88	11.16	7.67	6.16
Trade-weighted average	6.16	5.46	8.07	5.92	5.26
Minimum	2.57	3.61	4.84	4.44	3.70
Maximum	12.12	14.16	28.68	16.90	9.57
Standard deviation	3.91	3.82	9.10	4.22	2.52
Implicit nominal tariffs[1]					
Agriculture	12.77	4.34	19.57	9.22	10.51
Food processing	11.38	14.75	30.09	18.26	10.52
Chemical industry	4.65	7.10	8.59	10.55	7.91
Light industry	14.97	5.24	8.44	8.45	7.01
Metallurgy	5.64	5.91	7.28	9.52	5.76
Machinery	7.44	8.77	12.70	7.40	8.07
Other	5.98	4.65	6.55	7.00	8.25
Simple average	8.98	7.25	13.32	10.06	8.29
Trade-weighted average[2, 3]	7.81	7.13	10.69	8.75	7.91
Without import surcharge	7.81	7.13	10.69	8.75	7.91
Minimum	4.65	4.34	6.55	7.00	5.76
Maximum	14.97	14.75	30.09	18.26	10.52
Standard deviation	4.03	3.64	8.65	3.82	1.74

Sources: National Bank of Hungary; Ministry of Finance; Ministry of Industry and Trade; and IMF staff estimates.
[1]The implicit nominal rate was derived by dividing actual tariff and duty revenues by (customs-based) imports.
[2]Includes import surcharge for 1995–97.
[3]The figures for 1997 and 1998 were derived from Ministry of Finance customs import projections in U.S. dollars and budgetary projections of revenues from tariffs and duties.

on a trade-weighted average, however, the overall implicit nominal rate stayed more or less constant at about 8 percent. Similarly, the average effective protection declined over the period by about 1 percentage point and followed the same pattern as the nominal (Figure 9.1). It can also be noted that the similarity in the path of both implicit nominal and effective rates between 1990 and 1994 could indicate that changes in nominal tariff policy were applied relatively evenly between sectors.

The share of imports in total production at basic prices (i.e., without taxes or import tariffs, etc.) increased over 1990–94 for every category in this study. This is an indication that even though the levels of protection did not fall significantly in this period, the economy was becoming more open in the sense that imports were playing a more important role in the structure of production. This is partly the result of a reduction in nontariff barriers over the period.

While changes in tariff policy might have been applied evenly over 1990–94, the sectoral structure of protection was, and remained, skewed toward the agricultural and food sectors. These two sectors show consistently higher nominal and effective protection rates over the entire period, and it is particularly noteworthy that the nominal tariffs in these sectors increased significantly in 1992. This increase was related to the switchover to market-based trade with the former Council for Mutual Economic Assistance (COMECON) countries. MFN customs duties were applied to trade with these countries starting in 1992. The chemical, machinery, and "other" categories show an increase in nominal tariffs between 1990 and 1994. It is also interesting to note that the dispersion of both nominal and effective protection, as measured by the standard deviation of the samples, diminished over 1990–94. In the case of nominal protection, the decline was over 2 percentage points, while in the case of effective protection, it was less (about 1.5 percentage points) but still noteworthy.

Conclusions

Hungary has made significant progress in the last few years in liberalizing its foreign trade regime as a result of unilateral measures and the impetus created by commitments to multilateral trade agreements, including the Uruguay Round and the EU Association Agreement. While authorities have, at times, resorted to measures to restrict imports, these measures have been gradually removed (in the case of the import quota and various statistical fees) or made less restrictive (in the case of global consumer quotas).

The disaggregated calculations in this chapter show that both implicit nominal and effective protection diminished only slightly between 1990 and 1994, but aggregate data show a substantial reduction of 5 percentage points in the average tariff between 1994 and 1998. The data also could be interpreted to imply that tariff policy was applied in a relatively even-handed manner between sectors during 1990–94. The agricultural and food sectors, however, continued to receive significantly higher nominal and effective protection than other sectors.

References

Cordon, Max, 1971, *The Theory of Protection* (Oxford: Clarendon Press).

GATT, 1991, *Trade Policy Review Mechanism: The Republic of Hungary—Report by the Secretariat* (Geneva: International Trade Centre UNCTAD/ GATT).

Nagy, A., 1994, "Import Liberalization in Hungary," *Acta Oeconomica*, Vol. 46 (1–2).

OECD, 1996, *Examination of Trade Policy Aspects Concerning Countries Requesting OECD Membership: Hungary* (Paris: OECD).

X Labor Market Developments and Flexibility

Reza Moghadam

Prior to 1990, recorded unemployment in Hungary was virtually nonexistent. Productivity levels were low owing to widespread disguised labor hoarding. The economic reforms that accompanied Hungary's transition to a market economy led to labor shedding and a sharp rise in unemployment (Figure 10.1). Is the level of unemployment indicative of rigidities in the labor market, or is it merely a reflection of other macroeconomic imbalances? Does the recent reduction in these imbalances bode well for labor market developments or are other structural measures needed? What do other indicators suggest regarding labor market rigidity or flexibility in Hungary?[1]

The Lost Million

The increase in the unemployment rate seriously understates the loss in employment as there has been a dramatic decline in labor force in Hungary since 1990 (Figure 10.1). Between 1990 and 1996, employment declined by as much as 1.5 million in Hungary, while unemployment increased from about 10,000 to about 500,000. What has happened to the lost million? This decline is not explained by any demographic changes in the structure of the population; the population of working age was roughly constant during this period at just over 6 million. The participation rate simply dropped, leading to a 1 million drop in the labor force. Unfortunately, consistent long-run series on the participation rate are not available. However, combining the data from the Labor Force Survey (only available since 1992) with data published by the Central Statistical Office prior to 1992 indicates that the participation rate fell by as much as 10 percentage points between 1990 and 1996.

It is important to understand the reasons behind the sharp fall in the labor force. A decline in the labor force may lead to lower productive capacity in the economy, particularly if the labor market is not flexible. The drop of 1 million in the labor force may have simply made explicit the fact that under central planning, these 1 million people were employed only in theory but not in practice. If so, then one would expect to see the participation rate in Hungary to be now in line with other countries. However, this is not the case (Figure 10.2). The female participa-

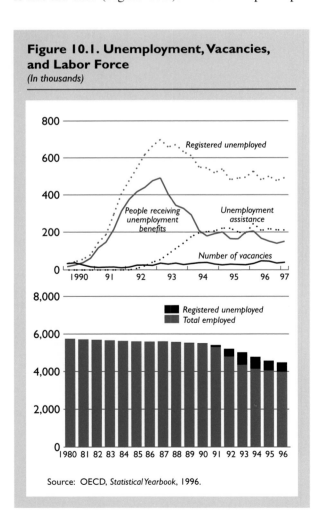

Figure 10.1. Unemployment, Vacancies, and Labor Force
(In thousands)

Source: OECD, *Statistical Yearbook*, 1996.

---

[1]For a more detailed analysis of the labor market in Hungary, see OECD (1997a).

Figure 10.2. Participation Rate, 1996
(In percent)

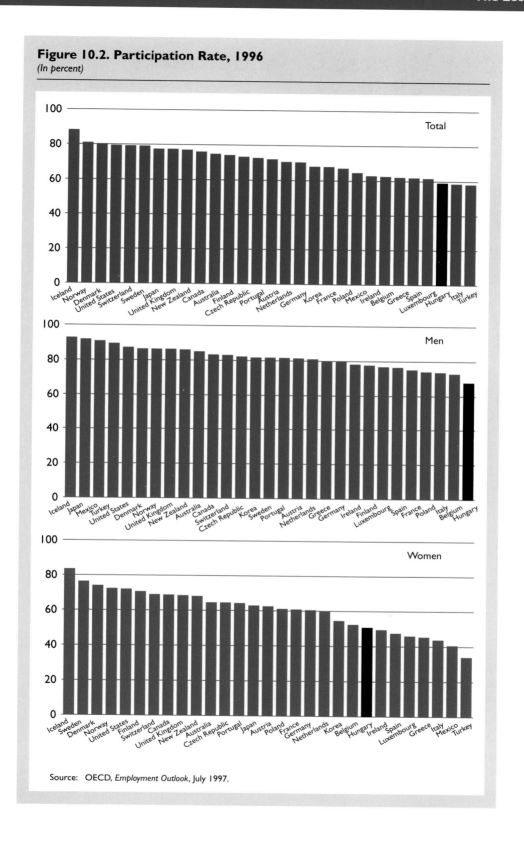

Source: OECD, *Employment Outlook*, July 1997.

Table 10.1. Changes in the Composition of the Labor Force, 1990–96
(In millions)

Decline in employment	1.5
Rise in unemployment	0.5
Decline in labor force	1.0
Of which:	
Decline in employed pensioners	0.3
Increase in income support, e.g., disability pensions but excluding unemployment benefit/assistance	0.2
Increase in working age pensioners	0.3
Other	0.2

Source: OECD, *Statistical Yearbook* of *Hungary*.

tion rate in Hungary is low compared with female participation in other OECD countries. More strikingly, the male participation rate is the lowest of the OECD countries.

Where are the 1 million people who left the labor force? Table 10.1 is a rough attempt at answering this question. One explanation is, of course, the "discouraged worker" effect. For example, between 1990 and 1996, the number of employed pensioners declined sharply—by about 300,000. However, other forces have also been at work. Besides unemployment benefits (see below), Hungary has an elaborate system of income support schemes, including disability pension, early retirement, parental leave, and sick pay. In addition, since 1991, Hungary has been developing active labor market programs. By 1995, about 20 percent of the working age population (or about 1.3 million people)—up from about 12 percent in 1990—received some kind of income support, including unemployment benefit (Figure 10.3).[2] The disability pension is the most common form of income support scheme, with Hungary having the second highest disability pension rate among OECD countries. Between 1990 and 1996, the number of recipients of this benefit increased from about 500,000 to 750,000 (see Chapter V for more details). About one-half of these individuals (those shown in Figure 10.3) were below the pension age. Labor market programs and early retirement have also become increasingly important. However, the number of those on sick pay has marginally declined.

The old-age pension system has also contributed to the decline in the participation rate in Hungary as can be seen by looking at the participation rate by age and across countries (Table 10.2). Until the pen-

___
[2]There may be some double counting here if individuals receive more than one benefit.

sion law was amended in 1996, the mandatory retirement age was 55 for women and 60 for men. Finally, another explanation for the decline in the labor force is the underground economy, which has partly been fueled by the high burden of taxation (see below).

Composition of Unemployment

Further insights on the causes of unemployment can be derived by looking at its composition. The Ministry of Labor and Central Statistical Office produce detailed data on the composition of unemployment by region, age, skill, and unemployment duration. Information on the unemployment-vacancy ratio (U-V ratio) is also available. What do these statistics tell us about the Hungarian labor market?

There is considerable regional disparity in the incidence of unemployment in Hungary. For example, in April 1997, the average rate of unemployment was 10.8 percent; however, it ranged from 4.9 percent in Budapest to as high as 20 percent in the Szabolcs-Szatmar-Bereg region. The regions with high unemployment tend to be those to the east, while Budapest and western Hungary have consistently enjoyed lower unemployment rates. This tendency is due to the following: first, prior to the transition, the heavy, and now obsolete, industries were based in eastern Hungary; and second, western Hungary with its proximity to Austria, and hence the European Union, has been an important beneficiary of inward investment.

In many European countries that suffer high and persistent unemployment, the rate of unemployment is high among the young, that is, those below 26 years old. This often reflects high labor costs or inadequate vocational or academic qualifications. In Hungary, the incidence of unemployment is also high among the young (Table 10.3); but it is not high by European standards, and it is much lower than, for example, in Belgium, Finland, France, or Italy. However, as in most other OECD countries, unemployment in Hungary is highest among those with low qualifications: nearly 80 percent of the unemployed have less than a secondary school academic or vocational qualification, and about 80 percent are blue collar workers.

The incidence of long-term unemployment in Hungary is rather high: over 50 percent of the unemployed have been out of a job for more than one year—well above the OECD average (Figure 10.4). Long-term unemployment is high among both men and women. There is considerable evidence that the long-term unemployed exert no pressure on wage inflation (Layard, Nickell, and Jackman, 1991). Therefore, long-term unemployment could reduce the po-

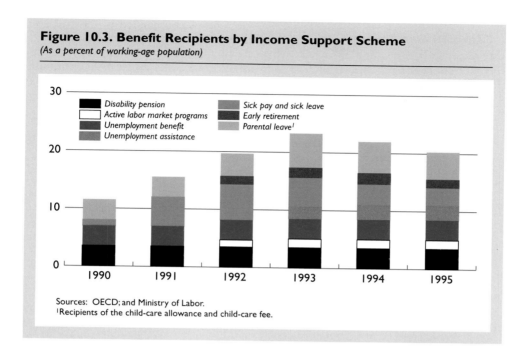

Figure 10.3. Benefit Recipients by Income Support Scheme
(As a percent of working-age population)

Legend:
- Disability pension
- Active labor market programs
- Unemployment benefit
- Unemployment assistance
- Sick pay and sick leave
- Early retirement
- Parental leave[1]

Sources: OECD; and Ministry of Labor.
[1]Recipients of the child-care allowance and child-care fee.

Table 10.2. Participation Rates by Age, 1995

	Hungary	Poland	Czech Republic	United States	Germany
Age group					
15–24	38.4	39.7	50.6	66.3	55.7
25–54	77.6	84.0	89.6	83.5	82.5
55–64	18.1	35.9	35.6	57.2	40.3

Source: OECD.

tential output of the economy through a higher natural rate of unemployment. In the presence of labor market rigidities such as employment protection legislation, a high minimum wage or high nonwage labor costs, and employers faced with continued uncertainty regarding future orders may refrain from recruitment for long periods of time, causing the persistence of both unemployment and, hence, high long-term unemployment. High fallback wages, for example, unemployment benefits, may also lead to high long-term unemployment through reducing search activity (see below).

In a typical industrial country, a rise in the U-V ratio would suggest a rise in structural unemployment. However, the U-V ratio in transition economies may not be a good indicator of structural unemployment because of significant structural changes taking place. Moreover, the number of reported vacancies may rise

partly because of improving collection and reporting practices. Finally, the official unemployment measure used here is based on registered unemployed, which may be higher than those who are actively seeking work. In any case, the U-V ratio in Hungary, after peaking at over 25 percent in 1992, has gradually declined to about 13 percent in early 1997.

Regulations and Constraints Affecting the Labor Market

To what extent can the high level of unemployment in Hungary be related to labor market rigidities? Below, several institutional elements are discussed, including unemployment benefits, the minimum wage, the wage bargaining system, and the taxation of labor.

Table 10.3. Distribution of Registered Unemployed by Age Groups
(In percent)

Month and Year	16 Years or Less	17–20 Years	21–25 Years	26–35 Years	36–45 Years	46–50 Years	51–55 Years	56–60 Years	60 Years and More	Total
December 1991	0.8	13.4	14.0	27.0	26.7	8.8	7.0	2.3	0.0	100.0
December 1992	2.6	9.4	13.8	25.9	28.2	10.0	7.8	2.3	0.0	100.0
December 1993	2.4	10.5	13.6	26.0	28.6	9.9	7.1	1.9	0.0	100.0
December 1994	2.6	11.5	13.6	26.6	28.0	9.5	6.4	1.8	0.0	100.0
December 1995	2.2	11.1	13.3	26.6	28.3	9.9	6.8	1.8	0.0	100.0
December 1996	1.6	8.1	14.1	28.1	29.1	10.4	6.6	2.0	0.0	100.0

Source: Ministry of Labor.

Unemployment Benefits

Unemployment benefits are provided through two channels: (1) unemployment insurance, which is financed through compulsory payroll taxes; and (2) means-tested unemployment assistance, which is administered by local authorities who pay 25 percent of the cost. Unemployment insurance is available for a maximum of one year, which is strict by OECD standards, and the replacement rate starts at 100 percent for those earning less than 6,000 forint a month (11 percent of the average wage in April 1997) and gradually falls to about 50 percent for those earning 36,000 forint (69 percent of the average wage) or more a month. In practice, however, the replacement ratio is much lower because of inflation: benefits are based on income during the last year of work. OECD (1997a) estimates that in 1996, the replacement ratio was less than 50 percent. In addition, the real value of the benefit has also been declining (by almost 25 percent during 1994–96). The conditions for receiving this benefit are also fairly strict: job separation must be involuntary (otherwise a waiting period is required); any severance payments are deducted from the benefit; and the individual must have worked for at least the equivalent of one out of the last four years.

Means-tested unemployment assistance is available for a maximum of two years, and is only available to those who are no longer eligible for unemployment insurance and whose per capita household income is less than 80 percent of the minimum old-age pension. The maximum benefit is also 80 percent of the minimum old-age pension, and all other income up to this limit is deducted from the benefit.

Wage Determination and Flexibility

Hungary has a national collective bargaining system whereby each year, discussions aimed at agree-ment on national wage guidelines are held by the Interest Reconciliation Council (IRC). The latter includes representatives of the trade unions, the employers, and the government. The agreement is nonbinding, but it is viewed as the floor for sectoral or firm level negotiations. Although the IRC agreement is generally applied in the public sector, actual wage increases in the private sector have exceeded IRC recommendation by as much as 5 percentage points. This partly reflects the increasing decentralization of the wage bargaining system (the number of national branch agreements affecting the private sector has declined rapidly in the last few years, and in many branches, wages are now decided directly at the firm level) and the fact that some rapidly expanding sectors of the economy (the financial sector, some sectors where multinational corporations are dominant) are not represented in the IRC.

The IRC also sets the minimum wage level, which the government then accepts and writes into law. About 5 percent of employees in Hungary earn the minimum wage, which is not particularly high by international standards.[3] Furthermore, the ratio between the minimum wage and average wages has declined by about 20 percent since 1990.

Nonwage Labor Costs

Nonwage labor costs and, in particular, employer payroll taxes have been widely identified as one of the key reasons behind high unemployment in a number of countries, especially of the young and low-skilled workers (Moghadam, 1994; OECD, 1997b). In Hungary, the tax wedge is high: in 1995, it was about 45 percent, the fourth highest in OECD

---

[3]About 8 percent of employees earn the minimum wage in France and 3.5 percent in the United States. The number for Hungary may also include some double counting because of more widespread practice of holding two jobs.

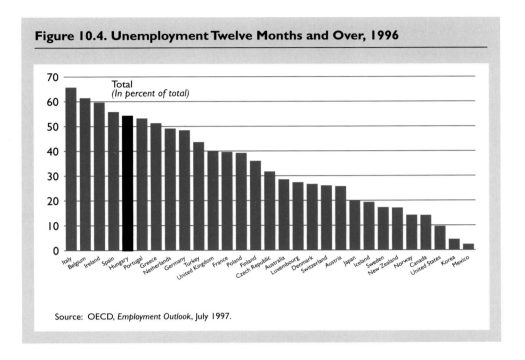

Figure 10.4. Unemployment Twelve Months and Over, 1996

Total
(In percent of total)

Italy, Belgium, Ireland, Spain, Hungary, Portugal, Greece, Netherlands, Germany, Turkey, United Kingdom, France, Poland, Finland, Czech Republic, Australia, Luxembourg, Denmark, Switzerland, Austria, Japan, Iceland, Sweden, New Zealand, Norway, Canada, United States, Korea, Mexico

Source: OECD, *Employment Outlook*, July 1997.

countries, against an average of about 33 percent (OECD, 1997a).[4]

Of course, a cut in labor taxes should increase the demand for labor. But would a switch from one form of tax to another—say, a cut in employer taxes and an increase in employee or income taxes—increase employment? From a theoretical perspective, the invariance of incidence proposition (IIP) implies that the replacement of an employer tax by an equal employee tax has no effect on the real economy, that is, the product wage, the consumption wage, and the level of employment will be unaffected (Layard, Nickell, and Jackman, 1991; OECD, 1990). However, this result may not apply, at least in the short run, if there are market imperfections—for instance, if wages are above market clearing values and adjust slowly, or wage negotiators care only about the "insiders." Even if the IIP holds, differences in tax liability could alter the allocation of resources. For example, employer taxes apply only to the wage, whereas personal or corporate income taxes also apply to income from capital. A switch from income taxes to employer taxes implies an increase in the overall rate of taxation on employment and a decrease in capital taxation, which may lead to a substitution of capital for labor. Similarly, personal income taxes are usually progressive, whereas social

security taxes are not. A switch from one to the other could lead to changes in the total tax bill for many individuals and firms and affect labor supply or demand decisions. Empirical studies (OECD, 1990) suggest that even when using a model where the IIP holds in the long run, a cut in employer taxes and an equivalent rise in employee taxes could reduce unemployment (OECD, 1986).

Whatever the theoretical considerations, there is a perception in Hungary that high payroll taxes are an impediment to job creation and a major contributor to the widespread incidence of tax avoidance. Realizing this, the government has been reducing employer social security contributions every year since 1995.

Other Institutional Elements

A detailed analysis of labor market laws and practices (OECD, 1997a) concludes that despite some strict employment protection and working time legislation in Hungary, there is no evidence that these institutional rules are particularly binding. For example, if a firm wants to reduce its workforce by more than 5, it has to go through an elaborate consultation exercise with the unions. However, most firms bypass this requirement by making redundancies in small groups over several months. Similarly, the standard workday is 8 hours and the maximum overtime hours permitted are 144 a year.[5] Overtime

[4]The tax wedge is the sum of employees' and employers' social security contributions and personal income tax as a percentage of gross labor costs (gross wages plus employers' social security contributions).

[5]This limit could be increased to 200–300 hours in collective agreements.

hours have to be remunerated at between 150 percent and 250 percent of the normal rate depending on when the overtime is done. However, most employers bypass these rules by not specifying working hours or by contracting out their work.

Conclusions

The significant structural changes that have taken place in Hungary during the transition to a fully fledged market economy complicate any assessment of the state of the labor market. Nevertheless, the above discussion supports the following conclusions. The flexibility of the Hungarian labor market has improved in recent years. Indeed, one could say that the Hungarian labor market is in many respects more flexible than several western European markets: in particular, the unemployment insurance system is one of the most strict in OECD countries in terms of providing incentives to search for work. Moreover, the reduction in the minimum wage in relation to average wages in the last few years, the declining weight of public enterprises, and the tightening of the budget constraints on the latter have increased flexibility in wage determination. However, together with the high unemployment rate, certain features of the labor market, such as high youth and long-term unemployment and low participation rates, do point to certain rigidities. One key impediment to job creation is high labor taxation, in particular high employer social security contributions. Although these contributions have been reduced in recent years, they remain high by international standards, and further reductions are necessary. Another key element that may hinder employment growth is the existence of a number of income support schemes that discourage labor market participation. The recent pension reform will certainly help in this area. Nevertheless, a fundamental reform of the disability pension system is also essential.

References

Layard, R., S.J. Nickell, and R. Jackman, 1991, *Unemployment, Macroeconomic Performance and the Labour Market* (Oxford, United Kingdom: Oxford University Press).

Moghadam, R., 1994, "Why Is Unemployment in France So High?" IMF Working Paper No. 94/58 (Washington: International Monetary Fund).

OECD (1997a), *OECD Economic Survey: Hungary* (Paris: OECD).

——— , (1997b), *Job Study Synthesis* (Paris: OECD).

——— , (1986, 1990, 1991, 1996, 1997c), *OECD Employment Outlook* (Paris: OECD).

XI Financial Markets in Hungary

Rachel van Elkan

Ten years after the initiation of reforms, Hungary has in place much of the infrastructure necessary for an efficient financial system that is well integrated with world capital markets. While the bulk of the legislative reform and institution-building were undertaken early on, the successful implementation of the 1995–97 macroeconomic stabilization program had a significant impact on the development of domestic financial markets. It contributed to a sharp increase in financial activity and improvements in the soundness of financial institutions. However, the financial system remains dominated by the banking sector: although activity in the domestic securities markets has accelerated rapidly, primarily in response to greater foreign participation, the size of the market for corporate debt securities remains limited.

This chapter discusses recent developments in Hungary's financial markets. Reflecting the dominant role of the banking sector, the discussion focuses primarily on that sector. The chapter then reviews developments in the securities markets and considers the effect of recent reforms on the future development of nonbank institutions. It also examines factors that may have held back development and competition in some areas.

The Banking System

A remarkable transformation has taken place in the banking sector since the establishment of the two-tier banking system in 1987. Burdened by an inheritance of nonperforming loans, and coupled with inadequate prudential regulations and lax supervision, the health of large state-owned banks deteriorated further in the early 1990s following the output decline that accompanied the transition process. Nonetheless, numerous small (mainly foreign or jointly owned) banks were able to compete successfully in this environment owing to their greater efficiency and the absence of a bad-loan burden, by skimming off the more profitable clients of the state-owned banks. Against this background, a costly se-

ries of state-financed operations were undertaken during 1992–94 to reduce the volume of nonperforming loans and to recapitalize the large state-owned banks. This chapter focuses on developments in the banking sector since the implementation of the consolidation and recapitalization programs, which laid the foundation for the recent extensive privatization of the banking sector.[1]

Structural Changes in Bank Lending and Deposits

Financial innovation, capital market liberalization, and the heavy tax burden on banking activities (including through reserve requirements) have contributed to a number of structural changes in the banking sector over the past four years, including a drop in the real level of bank credit and private savings in banks, an increased share of domestic bank credit absorbed by the enterprise sector at the expense of households, and a decline in banks' maturity transformation ratio.

The most apparent phenomenon affecting the banking system in the last few years was a sharp decline in the intermediation of financial resources. Between 1993 and 1995, bank deposits and bank-issued securities held by the private sector (noncash M3) declined by 10 percent in real terms (Table 11.1). During the same period, the stock of outstanding discount treasury bills increased from 12 percent of noncash M3 to more than 25 percent of noncash M3. Although some banking sector disintermediation would be expected from the introduction of nonbank-issued financial instruments, disintermediation was hastened by the heavy taxation of banking activities through the imposition of high reserve requirements (which peaked at 17 percent in 1995), coupled with low rates of remuneration (especially on reserves accumulated against forint-denominated deposits). As a result of these

---

[1]For a more extensive discussion of earlier developments in the banking sector, see Balassa (1996) and National Bank of Hungary (1994).

Table 11.1. Banking Sector Liabilities
(In percent; end of period)

	1993	1994	1995	1996	June 1997
Composition of noncash M3					
Deposits of nonbanks	84.3	84.4	83.2	82.5	83.9
Households	42.3	46.4	47.0	47.0	48.7
Of which:					
In foreign exchange	12.4	15.7	19.1	17.0	16.6
Enterprises	32.4	29.5	28.3	28.3	27.9
Of which:					
In foreign exchange[1]	7.6	6.0	8.2	7.2	7.0
Other	9.6	8.6	7.9	7.2	7.3
Bank-issued bonds and savings notes	15.7	15.6	16.8	17.5	16.1
Share of noncash M3 in foreign exchange (in percent)					
Households (including bank securities)	21.5	25.4	30.0	26.4	25.6
Enterprises	23.5	20.4	29.0	25.4	24.9
Memorandum items:					
Noncash M3 (in billions of forint)	1,645.2	1,868.4	2,296.2	2,848.7	2,921.1
Foreign exchange deposits (in billions of U.S. dollars)	3.3	3.7	4.5	4.2	3.7
Households	2.0	2.7	3.1	2.9	2.6
Enterprises	1.2	1.0	1.4	1.2	1.1
Real noncash M3 (1993 = 100)	100	93.7	89.8	92.9	84.5
Real household deposits and bank securities (1993 = 100)	100	100.1	98.7	103.4	94.5
Real enterprise deposits (1993 = 100)	100	85.2	78.5	81.2	72.7
Discount treasury bills as share of noncash M3 (in percent)	11.8	14.3	17.9	25.5	...

Sources: National Bank of Hungary, *Monthly Report*, various editions; data provided by the National Bank of Hungary; and IMF staff calculations.
[1]Enterprise foreign exchange deposits increased temporarily in December 1995 owing to the privatization of MATAV.

regulations, during 1993–95, banks gave up interest of 3–3½ percentage points on their forint liabilities (Figure 11.1). Following the decline in the burden of reserve requirements and the overall improvement in macroeconomic conditions in 1996, deposit-taking activities began to recover, with noncash M3 rising in real terms by 3½ percent. It is still premature to assess whether this increase marks a change in trend. In early 1997, bank deposits declined sharply once again, but this reflected bank-specific problems faced by Postabank, the second largest deposit-taking institution in Hungary. More recent data show that by mid-1997, real noncash M3 had recovered to its end-1996 level (in seasonally adjusted terms).

The deceleration in deposits was particularly strong for enterprise deposits, possibly reflecting the wider array of assets available to enterprises. Between 1993 and 1996, corporate deposits fell by 20 percent in real terms.[2] In contrast, real household savings held in banks increased slightly dur-

ing this period, as the domestic banking system maintained its position as the primary depository for household financial savings (Table 11.2). This was due in part to the regional monopolies held by the National Savings Bank and the 250 savings cooperatives, and to the relatively high per unit transaction cost associated with purchases of government paper.[3]

As to the currency composition of bank deposits, the share of household savings at banks denominated in foreign currency increased from 22 percent at the end of 1993 to 30 percent at the end of 1995, as households attempted to preserve the real value of their savings in the context of accelerating inflation and foreign interest differentials that discouraged forint saving. Moreover, the share of corporate deposits held in foreign exchange increased sharply in 1995 as enterprises were permitted (from April 1995) to retain their export proceeds in bank deposits, thereby avoiding the surrender requirement. The proportion of household and enterprise deposits

---

[2]The decline in corporate deposits accelerated sharply in the first half of 1997, as firms drew down their savings to finance their investment needs.

[3]The role of banks as a depository for personal savings will be buoyed beginning in 1998, when wages of public sector employees will be transferred automatically to bank accounts.

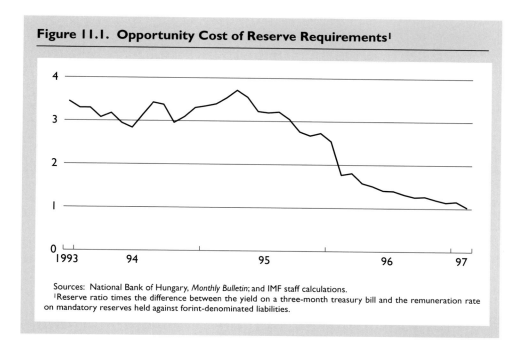

Figure 11.1. Opportunity Cost of Reserve Requirements[1]

Sources: National Bank of Hungary, *Monthly Bulletin*; and IMF staff calculations.
[1]Reserve ratio times the difference between the yield on a three-month treasury bill and the remuneration rate on mandatory reserves held against forint-denominated liabilities.

held in foreign exchange has, however, declined since the end of 1995 (to about 26 percent at mid-1997), reflecting the growing credibility of the crawling peg exchange system and (in the case of households) the relaxation of controls on the purchase of foreign exchange.

The contraction in bank deposits was mirrored by a decline in real bank credit (Table 11.3). This fall initially affected both credit to the government and to the private sector. During 1993–96, credit to the corporate sector contracted by more than 15 percent.

This contraction occurred in the context of capital account liberalization and was triggered by the large intermediation spreads of domestic banks (Figure 11.2), which made foreign financing relatively cheap. This tendency was reinforced in 1995 with the reversal of the foreign interest differential following the introduction of the crawling peg exchange regime (Figure 2.3 in Chapter II), which made borrowing in foreign exchange relatively cheaper. As a result of these factors, and the strong presence of foreign companies in Hungary, the share

Table 11.2. Household Financial Savings
(End of period)

	1993	1994	1995	1996	June 1997
Share of total savings held in					
Cash	21.7	19.4	17.7	15.9	14.5
Bank deposits and bonds in forint	50.9	46.4	43.5	45.9	45.4
Bank deposits in foreign exchange	15.0	17.1	20.4	17.8	15.8
Nonbank securities	8.6	13.8	14.9	16.4	19.3
Insurance premiums and retirement savings accounts	3.8	3.4	3.5	4.0	4.9
Memorandum items:					
Total savings (in billions of forint)	1,360.7	1,721.6	2,148.1	2,678.1	3,055.0
Share of household savings held in banks	65.9	63.4	63.9	63.6	61.2
Share of household savings in foreign exchange	15.0	17.1	20.4	17.8	15.8

Sources: National Bank of Hungary, *Monthly Report*, various editions; and IMF staff calculations.

Table 11.3. Bank Credit to the Nonbank Sector
(End of period)

	1993	1994	1995	1996	June 1997
Real bank credit (1993 = 100)	100	92.7	81.1	82.1	76.1
Government[1]	100	85.1	78.0	83.5	63.3
Enterprises (including small enterprises)	100	94.2	84.4	89.1	94.8
In forint	100	92.1	67.7	70.5	74.4
In foreign exchange	100	128.4	293.5	326.5	352.6
Households	100	94.2	68.1	52.9	42.9
Sectoral allocation of bank credit (in percent)					
Government	36.2	33.2	34.9	36.8	30.1
Enterprises (including small enterprises)	47.1	47.9	49.0	51.2	58.7
Households	14.8	15.1	12.5	9.5	8.4
Other	1.8	3.8	3.7	2.5	2.8
Currency composition of bank credit to enterprises					
In foreign exchange (in percent)	8.6	10.6	26.7	27.7	28.3
Enterprise credit in foreign exchange (in billions of U.S. dollars)	0.7	0.8	1.9	2.1	2.3

Sources: National Bank of Hungary, *Monthly Report*, various editions; data provided by the National Bank of Hungary; and IMF staff calculations.
[1]Including banks' holdings of government securities.

of corporate credit source abroad increased from 24 percent in 1993 to 44 percent in 1995 (Figure 11.3).[4] With the decline in domestic bank intermediation spreads in 1996 and the recovery in real activity, domestic bank lending to enterprises recovered rapidly, particularly during 1997. As a result, the share of corporate credit in total bank credit rose from 47 percent in 1993 to 51 percent in 1996, and to almost 60 percent at mid-1997. As to households, their share of bank credit declined slowly from 15 percent to 8½ percent, reflecting limited provision of mortgage financing following the termination of the state-subsidized housing loan scheme in 1991. The establishment in 1997 of the first mortgage lending institution is expected to relieve the credit constraints facing the household sector.

Maturity transformation by banks declined over the past four years. Less than 29 percent of short-term enterprise and household deposits and bank securities were transformed into loans in excess of one year in 1996, down from 39 percent in 1993. This may reflect improvements in banks' lending practices, which have reduced the tendency for "automatic" long-term lending to unviable enterprises. In addition, banks' ability to assess the creditworthiness of potential clients—especially start-up firms—

may not be fully developed yet, leading to greater caution in extending long-term credits. Finally, uncertainty about the pace of disinflation may have discouraged banks from locking-in long-term interest rates on loans when the majority of deposits are short term.

Market Structure, Competition, and Specialization

Despite several mergers and license revocations, the number of banks operating in Hungary declined only slightly from 43 in 1993 to 42 at present.[5] Seven of these banks have a market share (measured in terms of total assets) in excess of 4 percent, and 10 banks have a market share between 1 percent

---

[4]At the end of 1996, nearly one-fourth of foreign credit was due to loans from foreign parent companies to their Hungarian subsidiaries.

[5]Reflecting Hungary's liberal licensing regulations and the initially underbanked nature of the economy, the number of banks in Hungary increased sharply from 20 in 1990 to 35 in 1993. Most of these new institutions were foreign or jointly owned small or medium-sized banks. A new Banking Law, which came into effect on January 1, 1997, tightened regulations for bank licensing and imposed more stringent requirements on the qualifications of bank managers and members of the board. In particular, banks must hold at least Ft 2 billion in registered capital (double the previous minimum requirement that was set in 1991, and whose value has been substantially eroded), and the previous one-step automatic licensing process has been replaced with a two-step application for establishment and operation, which must be approved by the Banking and Capital Markets Supervision Agency.

Figure 11.2. Intermediation Spread[1]
(Three-month moving average)

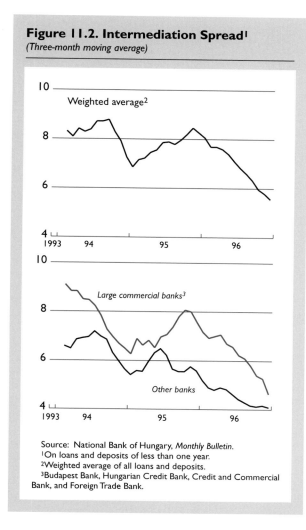

Source: National Bank of Hungary, *Monthly Bulletin*.
[1]On loans and deposits of less than one year.
[2]Weighted average of all loans and deposits.
[3]Budapest Bank, Hungarian Credit Bank, Credit and Commercial Bank, and Foreign Trade Bank.

Market concentration in Hungary's banking system continued to decline over the past four years, with the market share of the seven large banks falling from nearly 80 percent in 1993 to 70 percent in 1996. The main beneficiaries were the medium-sized banks, which have seen their market share expand by 8 percentage points to more than 19 percent of total assets. Concentration, however, remains more significant on the deposit market, particularly for retail deposits: the large retail banks (notably OTP and Postabank) still account for more than 80 percent of household deposits, largely reflecting their continued branch monopoly in the regions of the country.[7] As a result of this liquidity segmentation, these banks (particularly OTP) retain their systemic position as the major source of funds for the interbank market, while the large commercial banks remain the main borrowers in the market. Nevertheless, improved access to foreign credit by Hungarian banks has tended to weaken commercial banks' reliance on OTP.

The increase in foreign ownership of the banking system—especially of medium-sized banks (see next section)—has led to heightened competition in corporate banking. Large commercial banks (including the recently privatized banks) have seen their share of corporate loans decline by nearly 10 percentage points between 1993 and 1996, to 62 percent, whereas the proportion of corporate loans provided by medium-sized banks has risen by the same amount to 27 percent. Competition among banks for elite corporate clients (including multinationals and large Hungarian firms) has been active, leading to a sharp drop in intermediation spreads from over 9 percent at the end of 1993 to about 4 percent at the end of 1996 (Figure 11.2).[8] Spreads at large commercial banks have consistently remained above those at other banks reflecting, inter alia, a less aggressive approach to attracting corporate clients and higher operating costs. More recently, however, the margin between spreads at large commercial banks and other banks has narrowed considerably, which

and 4 percent. Five of the seven large banks are remnants of the monobanking system, which was disbanded in 1987.[6]

---

[6]The National Savings Bank (OTP) and the Foreign Trade Bank (MKB) existed under the previous system to collect household savings and to provide foreign-exchange related services, respectively. The other three banks that are remnants of the monobank system were established to assume the commercial banking activities of the National Bank of Hungary. The loan portfolio of the National Bank of Hungary was allocated to these banks on a sectoral basis, with the loans of the Credit and Commercial Bank (K&H) concentrated in agriculture, those of the Hungarian Credit Bank (MHB) concentrated in the chemical and machine-building sectors, and those of Budapest Bank (BB) concentrated in the coal mining and construction sectors. At present, the other two large banks are the retail-based Postabank, established in 1988 with the post office and the Ministry of Finance having the largest stakes, and the National Bank of Hungary and foreign-owned Central-European International Bank (CIB), established in 1979. Until 1997, the CIB operated as an offshore bank and therefore was not strictly part of the domestic banking system.

---

[7]A factor behind the continued dominance of these banks is the relatively high cost of establishing a branch network. While there are no legal restrictions on the establishment of branches by banks already operating in Hungary, the costliness of establishing such a network has so far acted as a constraint on competition. This said, the establishment by nontraditional retail banks of home banking facilities and automated teller machines, which obviate the need for a costly retail network, are expected to undermine the existing regional retail banking monopolies. Competition in the banking sector will be further enhanced from 1998, when foreign-operated offshore banks will be permitted to open branches in Hungary without having to establish expensive local headquarter facilities.

[8]Also contributing to the drop in intermediation spreads is the improvement in the quality of loan portfolios (see below), which reduced the need to generate provisions out of net interest income.

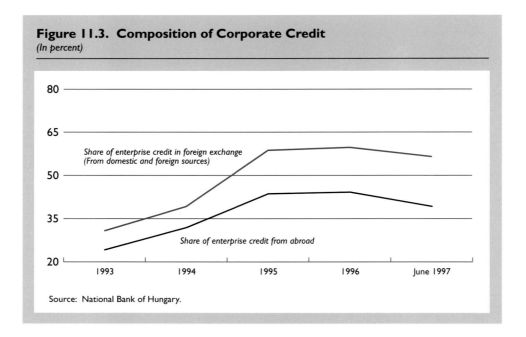

Figure 11.3. Composition of Corporate Credit
(In percent)

Share of enterprise credit in foreign exchange
(From domestic and foreign sources)

Share of enterprise credit from abroad

Source: National Bank of Hungary.

could reflect a more forceful approach to competition by banks' new foreign owners. Moreover, increased competition has contributed to a greater pass-through of changes in money market rates to lending rates in all banks.[9]

Ownership Structure and Privatization

Over the past four years, foreign ownership in Hungary's banking sector increased substantially. While the number of foreign or jointly owned banks rose from 28 in 1993 to only 31 in 1996 (out of a total of 42 banks), the share of bank assets under foreign or joint ownership increased from less than one-third to over three-fourths, reflecting the privatization of several large state-owned banks. Moreover, the share of foreign ownership in registered capital exceeded 55 percent in June 1997, up from 12 percent in 1993, and is expected to reach about 70 percent by the end of 1997.[10]

The increase in foreign ownership is attributable to several factors: privatization of state-owned banks to foreign owners; exit of Hungarian-owned banks and establishment of new foreign-owned financial institutions in Hungary; and foreign banks raising their equity capital at a faster rate than Hungarian-owned banks. With respect to the first factor, privatization of majority stakes in the large and medium commercial banks was carried out through strategic foreign investors in order to raise banking efficiency and to meet internationally based prudential regulations, and is the most important contribution to the increase in foreign ownership.[11] As a result, nearly two-fifths of bank capital is currently held by foreign *banks* (as opposed to foreign institutional investors).[12] Foreign investors were attracted to Hungary's commercial banks to meet the demand for banking services from foreign firms operating there, to establish a platform for operations in the region, and to tap the underdeveloped retail banking market. The relatively rapid increase in equity in foreign-owned banks is due in part to the requirement in several of the privatization

---

[9]Cottarelli (1998) finds that in Hungary, the effect on, and subsequent pass-through to, bank lending rates from a change in treasury bill yields is higher in the period since January 1994 than during January 1989 and May 1993. See also Világi and Vincze (1995).

[10]Owing to the 1993–94 state-financed bank recapitalization program, the share of bank capital owned by the State (defined as the Ministry of Finance, the privatization agency, and the social security funds) rose from 40 percent in 1992 to nearly 70 percent in 1993. With the privatization of the recapitalized banks, this share declined to 33 percent in 1996.

[11]Prior to 1995, the State maintained effective control of the five large banks that formed the basis of the domestic financial system. Bank privatization accelerated in 1995, with the privatization of Budapest Bank and the partial sale of OTP. In 1996, privatization of the Foreign Trade Bank was completed and Magyar Hitel Bank was sold. The privatization of a minority share of Kereskedelmi & Hitel (K&H—Credit and Commercial) Bank was concluded in July 1997.

[12]In contrast, a minority holding in the National Savings Bank was privatized through public share offerings, primarily to foreign financial investors.

Table 11.4. Quality of Banks' Loan Portfolios[1]
(In percent of total loans)

	December 1991	December[2] 1992	December[3] 1992	September 1993	December[4] 1993	December[5] 1993	December 1994	December 1995	December 1996
Problem free	90.6	83.1	88.9	86.0	82.5	71.5	77.5	83.1	89.0
Problematic	9.4	16.9	11.1	14.0	17.5	28.5	22.5	16.9	11.0
Of which:									
Under observation	0.0	0.0	0.0	0.0	0.0	6.5	7.8	7.5	5.9
Substandard	1.9	2.3	2.3	1.7	4.1	2.8	2.2	1.6	1.0
Doubtful	5.1	3.7	3.8	4.8	4.2	6.0	3.6	2.6	1.3
Bad	2.5	11.0	5.0	7.6	9.2	13.2	8.9	5.2	2.8
Memorandum item:									
Total loans (in billions of forint)	1,617	1,633	1,739	1,871	2,011	1,925	2,400	2,561	3,688

Sources: National Bank of Hungary; and IMF staff calculations.
[1]From December 1993, includes savings cooperatives.
[2]Prior to loan consolidation.
[3]After loan consolidation.
[4]According to 1991 classification rules.
[5]According to 1993 classification rules.

agreements that foreign strategic owners inject new capital into the banks.[13]

Bank Soundness and Profitability

The quality of banks' portfolios improved substantially over the past four years. While in 1993, 28½ percent of loans were classified as problematic and more than 13 percent were classified as bad, at the end of 1996, these ratios had fallen to 11½ percent and 3 percent, respectively (Table 11.4).[14] Several factors contributed to this turnaround. First, bank recapitalization and loan consolidation schemes carried out in 1993–94 replaced banks' nonperforming loans with government paper and injected sufficient capital to enable banks to fully provision against, and subsequently write off a large part of their problem loans.[15] Second, foreign owners instituted more prudent lending practices, and state-owned banks were required to implement restructuring programs to participate in the recapitalization schemes.[16] Third, increased profitability in the enterprise sector improved the outlook for corporate loans.

Reflecting the improvement in loan quality, banks at present are required to hold fewer specific risk provisions.[17] As a result, at the end of 1996, the level of banks' specific provisions declined to 3½ percent of total loans (one-third of classified loans), from 15 percent of total loans (one-half of classified loans) at the end of 1993. However, while the current level of risk provisions satisfies minimum prudential requirements, it falls short of the upper bound of existing provisioning requirements (see footnote 17) by about 14 percent of classified loans.[18]

In contrast to their management of specific risk, Hungarian banks have tended to adopt a more cautious approach to systemic risk, holding general reserves well in excess of the level required to achieve

[13]The State's legally mandated permanent shareholding in OTP was reduced from 25 percent plus one vote to a single golden share, following approval of an amendment to the Privatization Law. With the privatization and related equity injection in K&H, the State (as defined in footnote 10) will not hold a majority interest by the end of 1997 in any of the large banks inherited from the monobank system. A capital increase in Postabank in mid-1997 reduced the State's interest in the bank to 38 percent.

[14]Among banks that participated in the recapitalization program, the share of loans classified as problematic fell from 40½ percent in 1995 to 30 percent in 1996, with a larger percentage decline in doubtful and bad loans.

[15]The amount of government bonds issued to banks by the end of 1994 for recapitalization or to replace their nonperforming loans was equivalent to more than 100 percent of banks' bad, doubtful, and substandard loans.

[16]The effectiveness of these commitments was, however, weakened by the absence of quantitative performance targets, and sanctions for noncompliance. These so-called consolidation agreements were replaced in 1995 with preprivatization plans that corrected the earlier deficiencies.

[17]Current regulations require banks to provision against classified loans as follows: 0–10 percent, 11–30 percent, 31–70 percent, and 71–100 percent against their to-be-watched, substandard, doubtful, and bad loans, respectively.

[18]In addition, banks are required to provision against their off-balance-sheet items. Owing to the rapid growth in contingent and future liabilities, the size of off-balance-sheet items increased from less than 10 percent of the balance sheet total in 1993 to more than one-fourth in 1996.

the minimum mandated 8 percent risk-weighted capital adequacy ratio (CAR). Moreover, the average CAR has continued to increase steadily, rising from 11½ percent in 1993 to nearly 19 percent in 1996. Reflecting the impact of bank recapitalization, the CARs of large banks almost doubled in 1994 from below the minimum required level. Small and medium-sized banks have tended to maintain higher-than-average CARs.

Several factors explain the tendency to maintain CARs in excess of the minimum required level. First, the 8 percent "Basle Capital Accord" rule may not be sufficient in transition and developing countries, which have less stable macroeconomic environments. Second, according to the Bank of International Settlement's (BIS) accounting rules, government paper is accorded a zero-risk weighting. However, large commercial banks, in particular, hold a large stock of long-term, fairly illiquid government paper that they acquired during the bank recapitalization program. Owing to the relative illiquidity of these assets, a higher risk weighting could be applied, thereby lowering the effective CAR. Moreover, with the decline in yields on government paper, in the near future, banks may choose to switch their assets to corporate loans (this trend is already apparent in the first half of 1997), which carry a 100 percent risk weighting, again tending to lower CARs. Third, banks require a large amount of capital to finance their risky expansion into the retail sector.

The profitability of the banking system improved markedly during 1993–96, after-tax profits increased to 1½ percent of total assets from a loss of more than 6 percent (Table 11.5). The turnaround in profitability was due primarily to improvements in loan quality: the cost of accumulating specific provisions *within a given year* declined by more than 7 percent of total assets, while net revenues from reducing *previously* accumulated provisions rose by 1 percent of total assets. In contrast, the contribution from net interest income was quite modest overall. Prior to 1996, however, growth in interest income outpaced that of the income base (also a reflection of improvements in loan quality). More recently, increased competition contributed to an erosion in intermediation spreads and a decline in the net interest earnings ratio.

Despite the increase in private sector ownership and anticipated productivity improvements, the costs of banking operations have shown little improvement. The ratio of operating costs to net interest income and revenues from fees and commissions remained about 50 percent in 1993–95, and increased to 56 percent in 1996, while operating costs have risen continuously as a share of total assets, in both state-owned and private banks. The persistence of high cost ratios comes despite a 7 percent reduction in financial services employment between 1994 and 1996, and reflects the tendency for relatively high wage increases in the financial sector (relative to the rest of the economy). In addition, cost increases also reflect the improvement in the quality and the increase in the range of services offered by banks. Large up-front expenditures on much-needed technology upgrading and the installation of a network of automated teller machines also reduced profitability, but these costs should be recoverable through future productivity improvements. A major element in banks' costs in 1996 was the extension of branch networks. However, this extension will be sustainable only if the demand for banking services rises sufficiently to match the increased supply.

Bank Supervision

Against a background of improved portfolio quality and greater bank profitability, supervision of the banking system suffered from several shortcomings prior to the adoption of the new Banking Law on January 1, 1997. The deficiencies of the previous system were due primarily to the fractured nature of supervision and to a severe shortage of resources. Under the previous system, responsibility for bank supervision was divided somewhat arbitrarily between the State Banking Supervision (SBS) Agency and the National Bank of Hungary. Moreover, the securities operations of banks' subsidiaries were supervised by a separate agency, thereby precluding a consolidated approach to the supervision of financial institutions. These problems have been remedied under the new Banking Law by merging the two supervisory bodies to form a unified agency capable of supervising a universal-type banking system. The supervisory responsibilities of the National Bank of Hungary have been restricted to those areas related to the operation of monetary policy and the foreign exchange system. Banking supervision also suffered from a serious shortage of qualified technical staff, owing to insufficient revenues from fees collected from banks and the fact that employees were covered by the civil service pay scale. As a result, staff turnover was extremely high as employees of the SBS left for better-paying jobs in private financial institutions: thus, although faced with a staff ceiling of 120, the average number of staff at the SBS in 1994 was only 101. In addition, owing to inadequate funding, the SBS was unable to contract sufficiently with external auditors to fully compensate for its own staff shortage. As a result, bank audits were carried out infrequently, and on an ad hoc basis, with many banks never having undergone a comprehensive audit.

The new Banking Law addresses these problems by exempting staff of the supervision agency from the civil service pay scale—thereby enabling the agency

Table 11.5. Banks' Profit Accounts
(As percentage of average total assets)

	1993	1994	1995	1996
Net interest income	4.4	5.1	5.3	4.5
Fees, commisions, and other revenues, net	1.7	1.8	1.5	1.9
Operating expenses	3.0	3.3	3.6	3.6
Operating profit	3.0	3.5	3.2	2.8
Other revenues (including from sales of loans and reductions in provisions)	1.1	5.7	5.2	3.3
Other expenditure (including loan write-offs)	1.5	3.5	5.3	2.8
Net operating profit	2.6	5.7	3.2	3.3
Specific provisions generated	8.5	3.7	1.8	1.2
Extraordinary profit	–0.1	–1.2	0.0	–0.1
Pretax profit	–6.0	0.7	1.4	2.0
Tax liability	0.1	0.3	0.3	0.4
After tax profit	–6.1	0.4	1.1	1.6
Memorandum items:				
Average total assets (in billions of forint)	2,535	2,898	3,429	4,161
After tax profit (in billions of forint)	–154	12	37	67

Sources: National Bank of Hungary, *Annual Report*, various editions; and IMF staff calculations.

to match private sector salaries—and raises the fees the agency levies on banks. In addition, the staff ceiling was raised to 260. Concurrent with the improvement in funding, the new law requires the supervision agency to perform continuous off-site inspections and to undertake on-site examinations of each bank and savings cooperative at least once every other year. These changes, however, are quite recent, and thus their effectiveness has yet to be fully tested in the field.

Exchange Activity and Growth of Institutional Investors

The activity of the Budapest Stock and Commodities Exchanges, while still limited, has developed rapidly in the last few years, partly because of the increased importance of institutional investors.

The Budapest Stock Exchange (BSE) reopened in June 1990, trading exclusively in shares until the listing of government bonds and treasury bills in 1992. Following several years of stagnation, activity on the BSE was extremely heavy in 1996, with the volume of spot trading increasing by more than 350 percent during the year (Figure 11.4). Turnover of equities increased by 460 percent, while government securities (bonds and treasury bills) trading rose by nearly 300 percent. Underlying this performance was a sharp increase in foreign interest in the domestic securities following Hungary's admission to the OECD in mid-1996 and the upgrading of Hungary's international credit rating by several rating agencies. As a result, foreign investors account for 70–80 percent of the total turnover on the BSE.

While retaining its dominant position on the BSE, the share of trades accounted for by government debt declined to 54 percent in 1996 from 63 percent in 1995.[19] This was due in part to the continued decline in the interest premium on forint-denominated debt, and the growing importance of over-the-counter (OTC) trading in government securities.[20] Reflecting the lengthening of the maturity structure of public debt and the introduction of indexed debt, the weight of government bonds in trading increased at the expense of treasury bills.

Equities accounted for 42 percent of BSE trades in 1996, up from 34 percent in the previous year, and market capitalization of shares more than doubled from 6 percent of GDP in 1995 to about 13 percent of

[19]In contrast, trading in corporate bonds is almost nonexistent on the BSE, and OTC trading is also quite small. While this reflects the added riskiness of corporate debt during the transition period, several blue-chip Hungarian companies have established their creditworthiness by tapping the international syndicated loan market.

[20]About 47 percent of government bonds and 29 percent of treasury bill trades were transacted on the BSE in 1996. In 1995, the volume of government securities traded over the counter was 10 times greater than the volume turned over on the BSE.

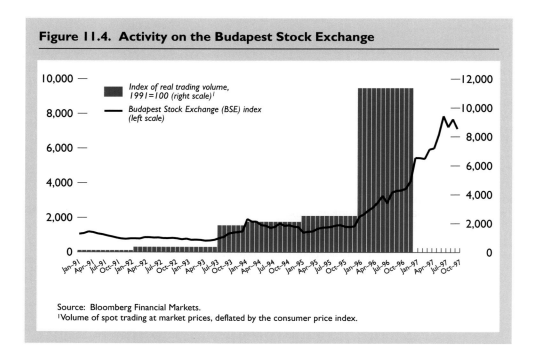

Figure 11.4. Activity on the Budapest Stock Exchange

Source: Bloomberg Financial Markets.
[1]Volume of spot trading at market prices, deflated by the consumer price index.

GDP.[21] While some of this was due to new listings (including the privatization through public offerings on the exchange of several strategic companies), the increase in capitalization reflected primarily an increase in prices. As a result, the Budapest Stock Exchange index (BUX)—which measures the performance of the top 22 shares ranked by market capitalization—increased by 170 percent in 1996 and by 133 percent in U.S. dollar terms, making the BSE the third best-performing stock market in the world (after China and Russia).[22] Nonetheless, capitalization remains small in comparison with industrial countries and the market remains thin, with only 45 equities listed on the exchange at the end of 1996 (up from 8 in 1990 and 42 in 1995).

In addition to the more traditional range of commodities, the Budapest Commodity Exchange (BCE) has offered financial contracts since 1993, primarily foreign exchange futures. Activity in these instruments increased more than 30-fold since 1994, following the introduction of the crawling peg exchange regime and the rapid expansion in foreign trade. In addition, while foreigners were not officially permitted to trade in foreign exchange futures prior to January 1997, it is likely that prior to that time, foreign investors in domestic securities

nonetheless covered their exchange risk locally through the exchange.[23]

At the end of 1996, the value of institutional investment reached Ft 360 billion (5½ percent of GDP), up from Ft 210 billion (3¾ percent of GDP) in 1995. Of this, 14 insurance companies accounted for the largest share (about Ft 210 billion), and the majority of their investments were in government securities. Investment funds accounted for Ft 128 billion, of which 55 percent was in open-end funds. Private pension funds accounted for most of the residual (less than ½ percent of GDP). While relative newcomers (the legislative framework for pension funds was established in 1993), the number of these funds has expanded rapidly. The popularity of pension funds, which may be organized on a regional, sectoral, or company basis, has been boosted by the income-tax exemption of this form of saving (since 1993). Following the phasing in, from 1998, of a compulsory fully funded component of the pension system, savings channeled through these funds are expected to increase substantially, with mandatory contributions projected to reach 1.2 percent of GDP in 2000 and 2.3 percent of GDP in 2003.[24] Moreover,

---

[21]In comparison, market capitalization of shares in 1996 in the Czech Republic and Poland was 35 percent of GDP and 6 percent of GDP, respectively.

[22]The BUX increased rapidly during the first seven months of 1997, although it dropped significantly during the second half of the year, following the worldwide decline in stock prices.

[23]Since 1995, the BSE has also offered futures foreign exchange contracts, but the trading volume has remained much smaller than at the BCE.

[24]Investment of mandatory pension contributions will be subject to the following restrictions: (1) up to 30 percent may be held in category A stocks listed on the BSE (corresponding to highly liquid stocks in the largest companies); (2) bank-guaranteed domestic bonds may not exceed 20 percent of total assets, while

since the preferential tax treatment of pension funds will remain in place, voluntary contributions to pension funds are also likely to continue to grow.

Concluding Remarks

Over the past four years, the Hungarian financial system has undergone a dramatic transformation. Within the banking system, the heavy burden of nonperforming loans has largely been eliminated, the majority of the sector has been privatized (largely through strategic foreign investors), and competition in corporate banking activities has strengthened. While profitability has improved on average, the banking sector will face a new set of challenges brought on by greater competition. These challenges will arise from the greater inroads into household banking by nontraditional retail banks, the increase in banks' exposure to more risky segments of the economy in response to the saturation of the market for elite corporate clients, and the greater capital and financial market liberalization agreed to in the context of OECD membership. These changes may well portend some further consolidation in the banking sector within the next few years. Financial liberalization, completion of the privatization process, and reform of the pension system will have substantial effects on other segments of the financial system. The privatization of additional shares in strategic companies through the BSE and the broadening of the range of foreign securities that may be traded within Hungary, together with the start of negotiations on NATO and EU enlargement, can be expected to increase trading on Hungarian exchanges. However, with the further liberalization of outward investment by Hungarians and the completion of privatization, interest in Hungarian securities may well subside over the longer term. Moreover, the gradual liberalization of outward investment by pension funds may also contribute to dampening activity on domestic securities markets.

References

Balassa, Ákos, 1996, *Restructuring and Recent Situation of the Hungarian Banking System*, National Bank of Hungary Workshop Studies, No. 4 (Budapest).

Cottarelli, Carlo, 1997, "Comments on the Paper by György Surányi and János Vincze," in *Moderate Inflation: The Experience of Transition Economies*, edited by Carlo Cottarelli and György Szapáry (Washington: International Monetary Fund and National Bank of Hungary).

National Bank of Hungary, 1994, "Consolidation of the Hungarian Banking System," *Monthly Report* (Budapest: National Bank of Hungary, October).

Világi, Balázs, and János Vincze, 1995, "The Interest Rate Transmission Mechanism in Hungary (1991–94)," paper presented at the conference on Hungary: Towards a Market Economy, held in Budapest on October 20–21, 1995, at the Hungarian Academy of Sciences.

---

foreign bonds may not exceed 5 percent of assets; and (3) investments in foreign equities issued by firms registered in OECD countries are permitted up to a ceiling of 10 percent until 2000, and 20 percent thereafter. No limits will be placed on holdings of government securities.

XII Foreign Borrowing and Capital Market Liberalization

Rachel van Elkan[1]

During 1993–95, Hungary was an active partici-
pant in international capital markets, borrowing on average about 11½ percent of GDP (in gross
terms). The amount of foreign borrowing recently
declined sharply, to about 3¾ percent of GDP in the
first half of 1997. This turnaround is most evident in
the case of sovereign borrowing, reflecting, in part,
Hungary's reduced need for official financing following the marked improvement in its current account and strong inflows of privatization-related
FDI. In addition, the relaxation of capital account restrictions has permitted increased access by the private sector to foreign capital, while also allowing
greater outflows of domestic capital. This chapter
discusses Hungary's participation in international financial markets during 1993–97, focusing on
changes in the cost and maturity of borrowing, and
the increasing role of private financing. It also docu-
ments progress with liberalizing capital movements
during the period.

Participation in International Capital Markets Since 1993

Between 1993 and mid-1997, gross inflows to
Hungary through international capital markets
amounted to $19.3 billion (55 percent in the form of
bonds), of which $12.6 billion represents sovereign
borrowing by the National Bank of Hungary (Table
12.1). During this period, there was a marked change
in the type of borrower and in the financial instruments used. While the National Bank of Hungary accounted for three-fourths of total foreign borrowing
during 1993–95, this proportion dropped to under
one-third in 1996 and to one-fourth in the first half
of 1997. Moreover, reflecting the partial withdrawal
of the National Bank of Hungary from capital mar-

kets and restrictions on private sector international
bond issues, the share of borrowing in the form of
loans from foreign banks increased substantially,
from 13 percent in 1993 to 90 percent in 1996, then
dropping slightly to 75 percent in the first half of
1997.

The gradual withdrawal of the National Bank of
Hungary from international capital markets reflects
the reduced need for official financing owing to improvements in the current account position and
large inflows of privatization-related FDI.[2] This recovery in the external accounts, together with Hungary's progress toward macroeconomic stabilization, made possible the upgrading of Hungary's
sovereign debt to investment grade by major rating
agencies in 1996 (see below). This upgrading, together with the general improvement in financial
market conditions for emerging markets following
the Mexico crisis, also served to improve borrowing conditions for the private sector. Moreover,
with interest rates on domestic currency credits
above those on devaluation-adjusted foreign currency loans and a dearth of domestic sources of
long-term credit, borrowing from foreign banks by
the private sector became an attractive alternative
to domestic sources of credit.

Capital Market Activities of the National Bank of Hungary

Between 1993 and mid-1997, the National Bank
of Hungary issued 42 international bonds in 12 different currencies, raising more than $10 billion,
compared with only seven syndicated loans, which
generated less than $2 billion.[3] The National Bank
of Hungary's reliance on the bond market during
this period reflected the tightness of the global syn-

---

[1]The author gratefully acknowledges the assistance of the Research Department of the International Monetary Fund in providing some of the data for this chapter.

[2]The government has not been active in foreign capital markets.
[3]The remaining two bonds were issued by the then fully state-
owned Foreign Trade Bank (MKB).

Table 12.1. Foreign Borrowing by Hungarian Entities
(In millions of U.S. dollars)

	1993	1994	1995	1996	Jan.–June 1997
Total	5,540	3,305	5,446	3,350	1,699
(As percent of GDP)	14.4	8.0	12.3	7.6	3.7
Bonds	4,801	1,729	3,311	333	414
Loans	739	1,576	2,135	3,017	1,285
Of which:					
National Bank of Hungary	0	475	848	650	0
Private corporations	411	256	528	911	...
Banks	30	335	269	671	...
Other[1]	298	511	489	785	...

Source: Capital data.

[1]Includes central government, local authorities, public corporations, utilities, and private finance companies.

dicated loan market for sovereign debt in the aftermath of the Paris Club debt renegotiations of the early 1990s, and the fact that the Japanese Credit Rating Agency (JCR) maintained its rating of National Bank of Hungary bonds at investment grade throughout this period. Accordingly, nearly one-half of total bond issues by the National Bank of Hungary between 1993 and mid-1997 were effected in Japanese yen, with deutsche mark accounting for about 30 percent of bond issues.[4] The majority of the funds generated through bond issues were borrowed at fixed rates, with only two issues linked to the London interbank offered rate (LIBOR).

Interest rate spreads at launch relative to benchmark sovereign bonds have dropped significantly since mid-1995, falling from an average of 227 basis points during 1993 to the end of March 1995 (when the austerity program was introduced), to an average of 190 basis points subsequently. The spread was just 90 basis points for the floating rate deutsche mark bond issued in mid-1996. This improvement in borrowing conditions reflected the upgrading of Hungary's debt by major credit rating agencies since mid-1996,[5] and the sharp compression in spreads in all high yield markets that is attributable to increased liquidity in global capital markets. The improvement in spreads on National Bank of Hungary bonds is also evident in the secondary market. In January 1995, owing to the Mexi-

can financial crisis and Hungary's burgeoning need for external financing, the interest premium on U.S. dollar-denominated National Bank of Hungary bonds in secondary markets reached 350–400 basis points in January 1995, but fell to 80–120 basis points in December 1996. Similar movements in secondary market spreads are also evident for deutsche mark-denominated bonds.

Although overshadowed by its activities on the international bond market, the National Bank of Hungary nonetheless remains the single largest Hungarian borrower in the international loan market, accounting for about one-fourth of total fundraising by Hungarian entities from foreign banks in recent years. This borrowing is a relatively recent phenomenon; the National Bank of Hungary entered the syndicated loan market in early 1994 for the first time since the late 1980s. Spreads in this market have also declined. The margin above LIBOR on U.S. dollar loans fell from 187.5 basis points in early 1994 to 20 basis points at the end of 1996.

The significantly reduced borrowing need and the increased capital market activity of the private sector allowed the National Bank of Hungary to play a less active role in international financial markets during 1996–97. Underlying this activity is the attempt to smooth the amortization profile of debt to avoid a clustering of repayments; to extend the average maturity of debt; and to refinance existing debt on more favorable terms. Accordingly, the Na-

---

[4]To limit its foreign exchange exposure, the National Bank of Hungary on behalf of the Ministry of Finance aligns through currency swaps the composition of its foreign exchange liabilities with the currency basket to which the forint is pegged.

[5]IBCA Ltd. assigned a BBB-rating in April 1996 for long-term foreign currency sovereign debt. Standard and Poor's (S&P)

awarded a similar rating in October 1996. Moody's lifted the sovereign debt rating to Baa3 in December 1996. At the end of 1996, Hungary's sovereign debt was rated below that of the Czech Republic and Slovenia by S&P, Moody's, and IBCA Ltd.; below Poland by IBCA Ltd.; and on a par with Poland and Croatia by S&P and Moody's. In June 1997, IBCA Ltd. further upgraded Hungary to BBB (the same level as Poland and Estonia).

tional Bank of Hungary prepaid about $1.5 billion in 1995 and a further $1 billion in 1996–97. In addition, about 90 percent of bond issues in 1995–96 had maturities in excess of five years, up from 80 percent in the previous two years. As a result, the average maturity of National Bank of Hungary debt has risen to 4½ years.

Capital Market Activities of the Nonsovereign Sector

Private sector borrowing from international capital markets has been limited to bank loans, owing to the National Bank of Hungary's failure to grant licenses for issuing foreign bonds to nonsovereign entities. Foreign loans to Hungarian banks and private corporations increased by more than 250 percent during 1993–96 to about $1.6 billion in 1996, reflecting the pickup in economic activity and the increase in the creditworthiness of the private sector. Total borrowing by these entities since 1993 exceeded $3.5 billion, of which 60 percent represents borrowing by private corporations. In the case of domestic subsidiaries of foreign companies (e.g., GE Tungsram), access to foreign bank credit has been facilitated by the established relationship between the foreign parent company and its bank, which helped to overcome the illiquidity in global loan markets in the mid-1990s. In addition, foreign and joint-venture banks as well as large commercial banks have continued to rely heavily on foreign loans as a source of funds, owing to their weak deposit base. Borrowing by public corporations, utilities, and local governments has also grown rapidly, reaching $0.8 billion in 1996. Utility companies, particularly MATAV and MOL, have been the major borrowers in this group, both in terms of amount borrowed and size of loans. In April 1997, MOL received a loan of $500 million, the largest single syndicated loan to a nonsovereign borrower to date.

Interest rate spreads on loans (including to the National Bank of Hungary) have declined rapidly; average spreads over LIBOR narrowed from 175 basis points in 1995 to 87 basis points in 1996. Moreover, reflecting the stronger profitability of the sector, the interest premium on loans to most commercial banks declined from about 25 basis points above rates paid by the National Bank of Hungary in 1994 to levels similar to those currently paid by the Central Bank. Premia on loans to utilities have also narrowed sharply; in the case of MATAV, the spread declined from 130 basis points in January 1996 to 30 basis points at the end of 1996, while the interest spread levied on loans to

MOL fell from 150 basis points in mid-1995 to 30 basis points in April 1997.

Capital Account Liberalization

Capital account transactions by the private sector were governed by the Law Decree on Foreign Exchange.[6] Under the law, financial institutions were required to report all foreign borrowing to the National Bank of Hungary, and foreign borrowing by other legal entities and the extension of foreign credits by Hungarian banks were subject to approval by the National Bank of Hungary. For nonfinancial entities, borrowing at rates in excess of LIBOR plus 2 percentage points was not generally permitted.[7] Over time, these provisions were interpreted more liberally, and the approval requirement on foreign borrowing was used primarily by the National Bank of Hungary to monitor foreign borrowing activity.

Access to Hungary's capital markets by foreigners was liberalized substantially in March 1994, when foreigners were permitted to purchase domestic government bonds in both primary and secondary markets, subject to the approval of the National Bank of Hungary for each individual bond series. Moreover, foreigners were permitted (subject to National Bank of Hungary approval) since September 1994 to purchase 12-month discount treasury bills and government bonds with a residual maturity of at least 365 days.[8] However, outward portfolio investments by nonbank residents were prohibited.

As part of its accession to the OECD, Hungary implemented a series of capital account liberalization measures beginning in 1996. Under the new Foreign Exchange Law effective January 1996, the approval requirement on foreign borrowing by Hungarian companies was lifted for loans with maturities in excess of one year; foreigners were no longer required to seek the National Bank of Hungary's permission to purchase Hungarian securities with maturities in excess of one year; and Hungarians were permitted to invest abroad (without approval) if they acquired an equity share of at least

---

[6]Since January 1996, these transactions are subject to the regulations of the Act on Foreign Exchange.

[7]In addition, loans could not exceed three times the registered capital of the borrower, and approval was denied for credit lines, revolving credits, and multicurrency options.

[8]Restrictions on banking activity have also been relaxed subject to the maintenance of controls to ensure sufficient liquidity in case of strong demand for foreign exchange. Domestic banks were permitted to grant credits to foreigners, subject to Central Bank permission if the credit was for more than one year. Banks were also permitted to buy securities from abroad with a maturity of less than one year.

10 percent in a foreign company based in an OECD member country. Further liberalization measures in July 1996 included permitting foreigners to buy Hungarian securities with an original maturity of 365 days or longer, regardless of the residual maturity, and allowing bonds and shares issued by OECD governments and companies registered in OECD countries with a AAA credit rating to be sold in Hungary.[9]

The following additional measures are planned for 1998: (1) permitting the operation in Hungary of branches of foreign companies; (2) allowing Hungar-ian individuals to raise credits in foreign currency from abroad provided the maturity is longer than one year (currently, such transactions are permitted for resident enterprises only); (3) permitting residents to purchase all shares, bonds, and other debt securities of OECD-based enterprises, regardless of their credit rating, provided the maturity is longer than one year, and allowing foreigners to issue such securities in Hungary (if denominated in foreign currency) without foreign exchange permission; (4) allowing residents to raise credits from foreigners in local currency with a maturity exceeding one year with the authorization of the National Bank of Hungary;[10] and (5) permitting residents to purchase real estate located abroad (residents would be required to report transactions to the foreign exchange authority).

[9]In January 1997, this latter condition was relaxed further to allow the sale within Hungary of shares and negotiable securities of any OECD-based company with an investment-grade rating. In addition, trading by foreigners in futures BUX contracts of 3 to 12 months at the Budapest Stock Exchange was permitted, and the minimum one-year maturity requirement for foreign investments was removed for banks trading in investment grade securities issued in OECD countries.

[10]Such credits can be financed by drawing down balances in a foreigner's convertible local currency account held at an authorized credit institution in Hungary.

XIII   A Look Ahead

Carlo Cottarelli

In view of the impressive accomplishments of the Hungarian economy over the last three years, one might conclude that the transition is by and large complete. In one sense, this is true: virtually all the institutional features of a planned economy have been removed, the role of the State has been greatly reduced, and the economy seems to have overcome the imbalances that had resulted from the transition process. As the European Commission stated in its opinion concerning Hungary's application for membership to the European Union:

> Hungary is a functioning market economy. Liberalization and privatization have progressed considerably, and there has been strong growth of new private firms . . . . Hungary should be well able to cope with competitive pressure and market forces within the Union in the medium term, provided the macroeconomic conditions for strong investment growth remain in place.

Moreover, according to the most recent EBRD, transition report (EBRD, 1997), Hungary now ranks first in all 11 indexes of progress in transition.

Even though the transition toward establishing a market economy has been successfully completed, much remains to be done to consolidate the results achieved, reduce the risks of external shocks to which a small open economy is typically exposed, and bridge the gap with Western European economies. Narrowing this gap will have to be at the heart of the authorities' strategic agenda for the next few years to set the basis for Hungary's eventual accession in the European Union.

This agenda will be as challenging as the last one, but will involve a change in the tactical targets pursued by the authorities. Hungary's external imbalance (as measured by the external current account) has now been brought down to a level that is sustainable over the medium term (Chapter III). The main objective in this area is to consolidate the results achieved in the past. If the external deficit is maintained at a level that is fully financed by foreign direct investment, the net external debt-to-GDP ratio will continue to decline from current levels, and reinforce Hungary's resilience in the face of external shocks.

With the focus of the external strategy shifting from deficit reduction to stabilization, another economic policy target is likely to come to the fore: inflation reduction. Inflation needs to be brought down decisively into the lower single-digit range—higher inflation would hamper Hungary's medium-term growth prospects (Chapter VII). The chances of a fast disinflation are good (e.g., a reduction in the inflation rate of 4–5 percentage points a year). The authorities' credibility in implementing macroeconomic adjustment has been established; a strong supply response is in progress and is expected to continue over the medium term; the strengthening of the external accounts will allow a more aggressive use of the exchange rate anchor; the solvency of public finances has been restored; and the increased flexibility of the banking system makes nominal interest rates more likely to move downward in line with the deceleration of inflation. In these circumstances, the tightening in the growth rate of nominal variables (the growth rate of money, the depreciation rate) that is required by disinflation, is likely to involve limited output costs. The authorities' achievement of the inflation target for 1998 (13½ percent on average and even less by the end of the year) would be an important step toward disinflation.[1]

Reducing inflation, maintaining a sustainable external position, and allowing growth of the private sector will require the continuation of the prudent fiscal policies that have characterized 1995–97. Structural reform of public finances will have to continue. The burden of taxation (including social security contributions) should be lowered further, a key step to stimulate the growth of employment in the private sector, which has remained sluggish even recently. Public employment remains high and could be further trimmed down. Subsidies to enterprises are still excessive, and further steps are needed to reform the welfare state. The distortionary and poorly targeted

---

[1]See Cottarelli and Szapáry (1998) for a discussion of disinflation in transition countries, particularly in Hungary.

disability pension system requires urgent reform. The health system has to become more cost-effective through the introduction of appropriate economic incentives to allow an improvement in the services provided to the population in the medium term.

An effort in the above-mentioned areas would be important in itself and a way of accelerating the process of convergence of per capita income to western European levels. Before the Second World War, Hungary's per capita income was about two-thirds of the average in western Europe. As an unwelcome legacy of the planned-economy system, by 1995, relative per capita income had dropped to about one-third of the western European average (Fischer, Sahay, and Végh, 1996). Since then, the au-

thorities' bold adjustment program has laid the foundations for a permanent reversal of this trend.

References

Cottarelli, Carlo, and György Szapáry (eds.), 1998, *Moderate Inflation: The Experience of Transition Economies* (Washington: International Monetary Fund and National Bank of Hungary).

European Bank for Reconstruction and Development, 1997, *Transition Report 1997* (London: European Bank for Reconstruction and Development).

Fischer, Stanley, Ratna Sahay, and Carlos A. Végh, 1996, "How Far Is Eastern Europe from Brussels?" (mimeo, International Monetary Fund).

Recent Occasional Papers of the International Monetary Fund

159. Hungary: Economic Policies for Sustainable Growth, by Carlo Cottarelli, Thomas Krueger, Reza Moghadam, Perry Perone, Edgardo Ruggiero, and Rachel van Elkan. 1998.

158. Transparency in Government Operations, by George Kopits and Jon Craig. 1998.

157. Central Bank Reforms in the Baltics, Russia, and the Other Countries of the Former Soviet Union, by a Staff Team led by Malcolm Knight and comprising Susana Almuiña, John Dalton, Inci Otker, Ceyla Pazarbaşıoglu, Arne B. Petersen, Nicholas M. Roberts, Peter Quirk, Gabriel Sensenbrenner, and Jan Willem van der Vossen. 1997.

156. The ESAF at Ten Years: Economic Adjustment and Reform in Low-Income Countries, by the Staff of the International Monetary Fund. 1997.

155. Fiscal Policy Issues During the Transition in Russia, by Augusto Lopez-Claros and Sergei Alexashenko. 1998.

154. Credibility Without Rules? Monetary Frameworks in the Post–Bretton Woods Era, by Carlo Cottarelli and Curzio Giannini. 1997.

153. Pension Regimes and Saving, by G.A. Mackenzie, Philip Gerson, and Alfredo Cuevas. 1997.

152. Hong Kong, China: Growth, Structural Change, and Economic Stability During the Transition, by John Dodsworth and Dubravko Mihaljek. 1997.

151. Currency Board Arrangements: Issues and Experiences, by a staff team led by Tomás J.T. Baliño and Charles Enoch. 1997.

150. Kuwait: From Reconstruction to Accumulation for Future Generations, by Nigel Andrew Chalk, Mohamed A. El-Erian, Susan J. Fennell, Alexei P. Kireyev, and John F. Wison. 1997.

149. The Composition of Fiscal Adjustment and Growth: Lessons from Fiscal Reforms in Eight Economies, by G.A. Mackenzie, David W.H. Orsmond, and Philip R. Gerson. 1997.

148. Nigeria: Experience with Structural Adjustment, by Gary Moser, Scott Rogers, and Reinold van Til, with Robin Kibuka and Inutu Lukonga. 1997.

147. Aging Populations and Public Pension Schemes, by Sheetal K. Chand and Albert Jaeger. 1996.

146. Thailand: The Road to Sustained Growth, by Kalpana Kochhar, Louis Dicks-Mireaux, Balazs Horvath, Mauro Mecagni, Erik Offerdal, and Jianping Zhou. 1996.

145. Exchange Rate Movements and Their Impact on Trade and Investment in the APEC Region, by Takatoshi Ito, Peter Isard, Steven Symansky, and Tamim Bayoumi. 1996.

144. National Bank of Poland: The Road to Indirect Instruments, by Piero Ugolini. 1996.

143. Adjustment for Growth: The African Experience, by Michael T. Hadjimichael, Michael Nowak, Robert Sharer, and Amor Tahari. 1996.

142. Quasi-Fiscal Operations of Public Financial Institutions, by G.A. Mackenzie and Peter Stella. 1996.

141. Monetary and Exchange System Reforms in China: An Experiment in Gradualism, by Hassanali Mehran, Marc Quintyn, Tom Nordman, and Bernard Laurens. 1996.

140. Government Reform in New Zealand, by Graham C. Scott. 1996.

139. Reinvigorating Growth in Developing Countries: Lessons from Adjustment Policies in Eight Economies, by David Goldsbrough, Sharmini Coorey, Louis Dicks-Mireaux, Balazs Horvath, Kalpana Kochhar, Mauro Mecagni, Erik Offerdal, and Jianping Zhou. 1996.

138. Aftermath of the CFA Franc Devaluation, by Jean A.P. Clément, with Johannes Mueller, Stéphane Cossé, and Jean Le Dem. 1996.

137. The Lao People's Democratic Republic: Systemic Transformation and Adjustment, edited by Ichiro Otani and Chi Do Pham. 1996.

136. Jordan: Strategy for Adjustment and Growth, edited by Edouard Maciejewski and Ahsan Mansur. 1996.

135. Vietnam: Transition to a Market Economy, by John R. Dodsworth, Erich Spitäller, Michael Braulke, Keon Hyok Lee, Kenneth Miranda, Christian Mulder, Hisanobu Shishido, and Krishna Srinivasan. 1996.

134. India: Economic Reform and Growth, by Ajai Chopra, Charles Collyns, Richard Hemming, and Karen Parker with Woosik Chu and Oliver Fratzscher. 1995.

133. Policy Experiences and Issues in the Baltics, Russia, and Other Countries of the Former Soviet Union, edited by Daniel A. Citrin and Ashok K. Lahiri. 1995.

132. Financial Fragilities in Latin America: The 1980s and 1990s, by Liliana Rojas-Suárez and Steven R. Weisbrod. 1995.

131. Capital Account Convertibility: Review of Experience and Implications for IMF Policies, by staff teams headed by Peter J. Quirk and Owen Evans. 1995.

130. Challenges to the Swedish Welfare State, by Desmond Lachman, Adam Bennett, John H. Green, Robert Hagemann, and Ramana Ramaswamy. 1995.

129. IMF Conditionality: Experience Under Stand-By and Extended Arrangements. Part II: Background Papers. Susan Schadler, Editor, with Adam Bennett, Maria Carkovic, Louis Dicks-Mireaux, Mauro Mecagni, James H.J. Morsink, and Miguel A. Savastano. 1995.

128. IMF Conditionality: Experience Under Stand-By and Extended Arrangements. Part I: Key Issues and Findings, by Susan Schadler, Adam Bennett, Maria Carkovic, Louis Dicks-Mireaux, Mauro Mecagni, James H.J. Morsink, and Miguel A. Savastano. 1995.

127. Road Maps of the Transition: The Baltics, the Czech Republic, Hungary, and Russia, by Biswajit Banerjee, Vincent Koen, Thomas Krueger, Mark S. Lutz, Michael Marrese, and Tapio O. Saavalainen. 1995.

126. The Adoption of Indirect Instruments of Monetary Policy, by a staff team headed by William E. Alexander, Tomás J.T. Baliño, and Charles Enoch. 1995.

125. United Germany: The First Five Years—Performance and Policy Issues, by Robert Corker, Robert A. Feldman, Karl Habermeier, Hari Vittas, and Tessa van der Willigen. 1995.

124. Saving Behavior and the Asset Price "Bubble" in Japan: Analytical Studies, edited by Ulrich Baumgartner and Guy Meredith. 1995.

123. Comprehensive Tax Reform: The Colombian Experience, edited by Parthasarathi Shome. 1995.

122. Capital Flows in the APEC Region, edited by Mohsin S. Khan and Carmen M. Reinhart. 1995.

121. Uganda: Adjustment with Growth, 1987–94, by Robert L. Sharer, Hema R. De Zoysa, and Calvin A. McDonald. 1995.

120. Economic Dislocation and Recovery in Lebanon, by Sena Eken, Paul Cashin, S. Nuri Erbas, Jose Martelino, and Adnan Mazarei. 1995.

119. Singapore: A Case Study in Rapid Development, edited by Kenneth Bercuson with a staff team comprising Robert G. Carling, Aasim M. Husain, Thomas Rumbaugh, and Rachel van Elkan. 1995.

118. Sub-Saharan Africa: Growth, Savings, and Investment, by Michael T. Hadjimichael, Dhaneshwar Ghura, Martin Mühleisen, Roger Nord, and E. Murat Uçer. 1995.

117. Resilience and Growth Through Sustained Adjustment: The Moroccan Experience, by Saleh M. Nsouli, Sena Eken, Klaus Enders, Van-Can Thai, Jörg Decressin, and Filippo Cartiglia, with Janet Bungay. 1995.

116. Improving the International Monetary System: Constraints and Possibilities, by Michael Mussa, Morris Goldstein, Peter B. Clark, Donald J. Mathieson, and Tamim Bayoumi. 1994.

115. Exchange Rates and Economic Fundamentals: A Framework for Analysis, by Peter B. Clark, Leonardo Bartolini, Tamim Bayoumi, and Steven Symansky. 1994.

114. Economic Reform in China: A New Phase, by Wanda Tseng, Hoe Ee Khor, Kalpana Kochhar, Dubravko Mihaljek, and David Burton. 1994.

113. Poland: The Path to a Market Economy, by Liam P. Ebrill, Ajai Chopra, Charalambos Christofides, Paul Mylonas, Inci Otker, and Gerd Schwartz. 1994.

112. The Behavior of Non-Oil Commodity Prices, by Eduardo Borensztein, Mohsin S. Khan, Carmen M. Reinhart, and Peter Wickham. 1994.

111. The Russian Federation in Transition: External Developments, by Benedicte Vibe Christensen. 1994.

110. Limiting Central Bank Credit to the Government: Theory and Practice, by Carlo Cottarelli. 1993.

109. The Path to Convertibility and Growth: The Tunisian Experience, by Saleh M. Nsouli, Sena Eken, Paul Duran, Gerwin Bell, and Zühtü Yücelik. 1993.

108. Recent Experiences with Surges in Capital Inflows, by Susan Schadler, Maria Carkovic, Adam Bennett, and Robert Kahn. 1993.

107. China at the Threshold of a Market Economy, by Michael W. Bell, Hoe Ee Khor, and Kalpana Kochhar with Jun Ma, Simon N'guiamba, and Rajiv Lall. 1993.

Note: For information on the title and availability of Occasional Papers not listed, please consult the IMF Publications Catalog or contact IMF Publication Services.